Bernhard Köppen
Norbert F. Schneider

Demographics of Korea and Germany

Population Changes and Socioeconomic Impact of
two Divided Nations in the Light of Reunification

Edited by the Federal Institute for Population Research (BiB), Germany and the
Korea Institute for Health and Social Affairs (KIHASA)

Verlag Barbara Budrich
Opladen • Berlin • Toronto 2018

A CIP catalogue record for this book is available from
Die Deutsche Bibliothek (The German Library)

© 2018 by Barbara Budrich Publishers, Opladen, Berlin & Toronto
        www.barbara-budrich.net
        ISBN   978-3-8474-2152-8
        eISBN   978-3-8474-1173-4

Das Werk einschließlich aller seiner Teile ist urheberrechtlich geschützt. Jede Verwertung außerhalb der engen Grenzen des Urheberrechtsgesetzes ist ohne Zustimmung des Verlages unzulässig und strafbar. Das gilt insbesondere für Vervielfältigungen, Übersetzungen, Mikroverfilmungen und die Einspeicherung und Verarbeitung in elektronischen Systemen.

Die Deutsche Bibliothek – CIP-Einheitsaufnahme
Ein Titeldatensatz für die Publikation ist bei Der Deutschen Bibliothek erhältlich.

Verlag Barbara Budrich (B:) Barbara Budrich Publishers
Stauffenbergstr. 7. D-51379 Leverkusen Opladen, Germany

86 Delma Drive. Toronto, ON M8W 4P6 Canada
www.barbara-budrich.net

Jacket illustration by Bettina Lehfeldt, Germany – www.lehfeldtgraphic.de
Cover image: fotolia.com
Typesetting: Sybille Steinmetz, Tim Aevermann, BiB
Typographical editing: Anja Borkam, Jena – kontakt@lektorat-borkam.de
Printed in Europe on acid-free paper by
paper & tinta, Warsaw

Demographics of Korea and Germany

Table of Contents

Index of Figures

Index of Tables

Preface

Similar to the Federal Republic of Germany, which did not recognize the GDR as a legitimate state in German territory, the Republic of Korea claims to be the political body for all of Korea and for all Korean citizens living on the Korean peninsula[1]. Given this context, the respective governments on both sides consider Korean reunification a fundamental concern. In the Republic of Korea, unlike in Germany, not only research and strategic analysis concerning the Democratic People's Republic of Korea (DPRK), but also scenario building and theoretical preparation for a possible regime change and Korean integration or reunification is conducted. Although the current tensions between the DPRK, the Republic of Korea and international sanctions due to hostile acts induced by the North Korean regime make a possible Korean reunification (and even the slightest rapprochement) rather unlikely, the case of Germany and the 1989/1990 revolutions in socialist Central Europe proved that changes can be unexpected and sudden.

In light of this, the Korea Institute for Health and Social Affairs (KIHASA) approached the Bundesinstitut für Bevölkerungsforschung/Federal Institute for Population Research (BiB), Germany to propose a joint research initiative on population changes and their socioeconomic impact before and after German reunification as a basis for Korean scenarios on "reunification demography" and as a starting point for institutionalized cooperation and research on topics of common interest.

This publication is the first tangible result of fruitful Korean-German cooperation by national government research institutes.

The production and finalization of this research would not have been possible without the support of researchers and student assistants at BiB in Wiesbaden and KIHASA in Sejong.

The authors would like to thank Prof. Dr. Sangho Kim, president of KIHASA, for initiating the joint research and cooperation with BiB.

Dr. Sam Hyun Yoo provided data and the chapter on the demographics of Korean reunification matters and Michael Mühlichen contributed the chapter on mortality and life expectancy as well as findings on post-unification demographics in Germany.

Dr. Tim Aevermann was responsible for administrative support, layout and all organizational matters concerning the practical exchange between KIHASA and BiB.

Sincere thanks also to Marie-Kristin Maaß and Robin Mohr, student assistants at BiB, Ingborg Beyer and Wiebke Hamann for support. Dr. Sabine Diabaté, Dr. Jasmin Passet-Wittig, Dr. Martin Bujard and Dr. Ronny Westermann at BiB have regularly contributed knowledge and expertise in discussions and reviews. Harun Sulak guaranteed data quality and provision.

Finally we would like to thank our partners at KIHASA Dr. Samsik Lee, Dr. Jong Hoon Kim and Dr. Sam Ling Lee who were important partners for fruitful discussions and relevant insights concerning demographic knowledge on South and North Korea.

Wiesbaden, November 2017

---

[1]   Conversely, the Democratic People's Republic of Korea considers itself legitimate rather than South Korea.

1   Introduction: Demographics of reunification

Korea and Germany are commonly described as emblematic examples of divided nations. In both cases, the post-World War Two political confrontation between competing ideologies caused the foundation of two states with very different societal and economic systems. For Germany[1], the fall of the Iron Curtain in 1989 and the union of the eastern German Democratic Republic (GDR) with the western Federal Republic of Germany (FRG) marked a new chapter in Germany's history as a reunified nation state (Figure 1).

The Korean Peninsula, in contrast, is still marked by severe division. Notwithstanding recurrent tensions as well as periods of reconciliation between the Republic of Korea in the south and the northern Democratic People's Republic of Korea (DPRK), the idea of an opening of the border and peaceful unification remains an important paradigm in both states. Hence, studies and scenarios on peaceful rapprochement and unification are an important and rewarding task.

Both, Korea and Germany underwent the fate of prolonged national division. Thus, it may be helpful to use Germany's past experiences of division and reunification as a source of reference points for Korea. Therefore, the Korea Institute for Health and Social Affairs (KIHASA) and the Bundesinstitut für Bevölkerungsforschung/Federal Institute for Population Research (BiB), Germany have joined forces to deliver the latest findings on demographics of reunification.

Demographic and socio-economic shifts as major challenges for reunification were discussed by Eberstadt and Banister (1992) from a distinctly Korean perspective. In our study, the German experience may provide knowledge and experience for further scenarios concerning the Korean Peninsula.

The unification of the two German states in 1990 was a unique venture and an outstanding achievement. There are certainly significant differences between it and the case of Korea and possible scenarios concerning the Republic of Korea, the DPRK and Germany's experience. Nonetheless, research on reunification is not only of scientific relevance, but might help to guide and manage similar events even more effectively and properly in the future.

The aim of our study is to provide profound thoughts on the impact that reunification had on Germany's demographics and in which parts of the population development trends or shifts could be expected in the case of peaceful opening of the inner-Korean border and abolition of the Demilitarized Zone, which separates the peninsula into two parts.

To do so, we provide a concise overview of selected and significant reunification-related population issues in Germany and later discuss whether and in what way the findings might be relevant for other reunification scenarios. Hence, as mentioned above, this study offers a demographic perspective of what changes the German transition has brought about and what lessons can be learned from a scientific point of view as well as from a policy and governance-bound perspective. Therefore, we also provide a brief introduction to the demographics of divided Korea.

---

[1]   Germany is a federation of 16 states, the so-called "Länder." The two virtual macro-regions of Germany, which were formerly the West German "old" Federal Republic (FRG) and the East German socialist German Democratic Republic (GDR) are often called either "Alte Länder" (Old States) and "Neue Länder (New States) or "West Germany" and "East Germany".

Figure 1: Federal Republic of Germany: Alte Länder and Neue Länder

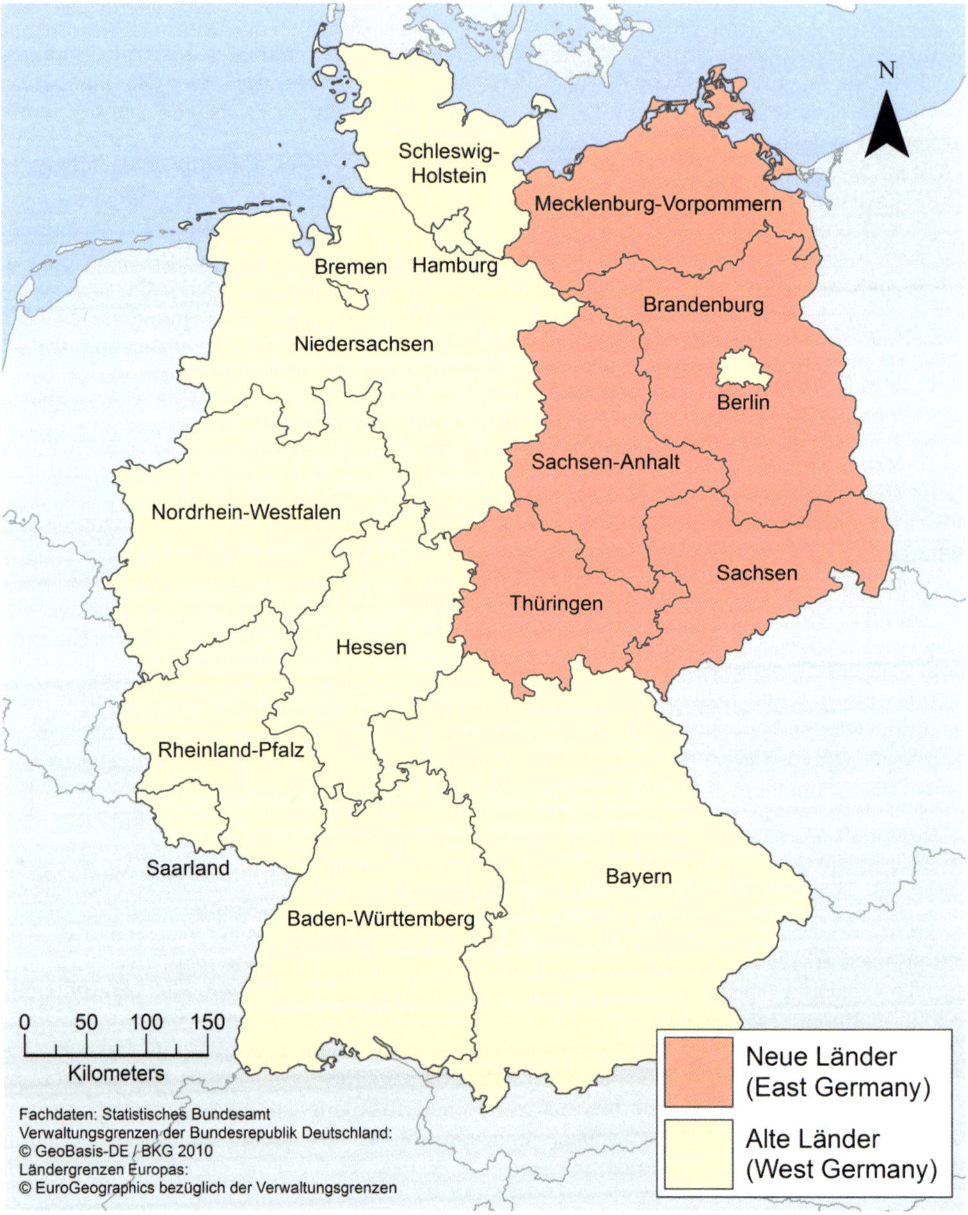

In this study, we focus on two central questions, one related to German demographics and reunification, the other referring to the possible transferability of particular experiences and findings for scenario-building in Korea under the premise of détente and mutual exchange between the Republic of Korea and the Democratic People's Republic of Korea (DPRK), either in the form of peaceful unification or a federation with open borders and mutual exchange.

The first question is relevant because in retrospect, 25 years after reunification, the initially very popular but simplistic idea of "catch-up modernization" in Germany has been proven erroneous. In fact, we observe convergent demographic processes as well as persistent "unique" East German and West German patterns. Therefore, we attempt to assess to what extent the observed demographic shifts are either purely unification-related, a result of catch-up modernization or linked to the 'general' long-term demographic changes of advanced societies/economies.

As for the case of Korea, our second question, we are fully aware that a collapse of the North Korean regime is not foreseeable and, due to the self-imposed isolation of the DPRK, extremely little reliable information is available about all of the spheres relevant to our research and scenario building. However, it is rewarding to study how reunification and demography in Germany relate. By doing so, we can isolate specific German occurrences from possible universal processes that come along with the merging of two different societies and transfer relevant knowledge into a scenario of Korean reunification. However, we do not aim to provide a blueprint for reunification on the Korean Peninsula, but versatile knowledge for scholarly discourse in reunification studies and quality-focused scenario techniques.

It is important to consider our approach a contribution with regard to the demographic impacts of national division and reunification, but not as a systematic cyclopedia of Germany's demographics since 1990. The spotlight is directed on those relevant variations in population development that occur in the context of national division and reunification. Hence, our study is rather specific and exploratory in character. It is a suggestion for interpretation and aims to encourage further discussion and research.

1.1   Theoretical setting

Studying German reunification and its demographic consequences, it is important to recognize that Germany did not actually experience a union of equals or the restitution of a formerly existing state. In fact, the GDR joined the Federal Republic of Germany after parliamentary decisions made in both states and having signed the treaty on German unification. This also means that as of October 3, 1990, the constitution (Grundgesetz), all legislation and the economic system of the "old" Federal Republic of Germany became authoritative for the "new" reunified nation. Hence, from a legal-administrative viewpoint, citizens of the Alte Länder did not experience any significant system shift, but the people in the Neue Länder experienced a complete regime change from one moment to the next (with yet unclear consequences at that time). The GDR was suspended and fully incorporated into the Federal Republic of Germany.

1.1.1 Modernization theory as early theoretical framework

Given this specific form of reunification, the rather simple idea of *"Nachholende Moderni-sierung"* (literally: catch-up modernization) as a universal pathway for the former GDR/Neue Länder was anticipated, but modernization theory as a core concept with regard to German unification soon proved unsatisfactory (Geißler 2002, Geißler 2014).

More than 25 years after reunification there is evidence that comprehensive catch-up modernization with convergence in all political, economic and societal spheres did not occur. In fact, the general increase in wealth and the rapid adaptation in political and economic terms are contrasted by a formerly unknown degree of social inequality and, for example with regard to female role models, de-modernization took place in the Neue Länder. The chief tendency towards modernization in the Neue Länder is, however, thwarted by countercurrents.

Theories of convergence are linked to the idea that modernization and globalization determine gradual, yet inevitable processes of homogenization. As a consequence, globally similar structures and cultural patterns occur. Differences between societies and cultures assimilate to a certain extent. National as well as regional specifics are also diluted or disappear entirely. This tendency is related to economic and technical innovations leading to more and more similar patterns of consumption. Therefore, cultural aspects are seen as less influential than economic aspects (Lewitt 1983). The above-mentioned patterns of consumption are distinctively of "Western" origin and have been commonly described as "McDonaldisation of society" (Ritzer 1993) or "Americanization" (Wagner 2001). According to this viewpoint, the leadership of Western, American-style culture is not only due to sheer economic dominance but also reflects the adaptability and general appeal of these products.

Fukuyama (1992) identifies the end of history with Western modernization as a (provisional) punchline with the end of state socialism. With this interpretation of contemporary history, convergence in the meaning of adaption of Western norms, standards and culture would be the foreseeable and inevitable path for the Neue Länder within reunified Germany.

1.1.2 Divergence and diversification: The appropriate way to look at German reunification?

With a special focus on population development, both convergent and divergent patterns can be proven when comparing the Neue and Alte Länder. Hence, another theoretical rationale comes into discussion: divergence and diversification. According to this approach, accelerated globalization makes people insecure and therefore individuals tend to oppose an increasing feeling of alienation and obscurity by reverting to regionalism.

Thus, increased tendencies of globalization may lead to more homogenous patterns of consumption, global norms and standards, but this does not inevitably change cultures at their core. Quite the contrary, globalization and modernization ultimately foster local culture and promote the (re-discovered) appreciation of regional specifics. Therefore, the postulated modernization-related global convergence and homogeneity is merely superficial (Huntington 1997). Radical responses to globalization and modernization lead to Huntington's claimed "clash of civilizations," because culture is understood as potentially immutable and strictly delimits one from the other. Intense contact with and the intrusion of one culture in another inevitably leads to friction and conflict. Current populist right wing and ultra-conservative movements in North America and Europe with distinct anti-globalization sentiments may serve as further proof of this theoretical viewpoint. Advocates of the convergence theory, however, would argue that these movements are especially attractive for the "losers of modernization" and will also vanish as time goes by (and modernization prevails).

Another far less alarming and oppressive variety of this theoretical framework puts emphasis on the idea of parallel, "multiple modernities" (Eisenstadt 2005). Thus, new diversity is embedded in the contrast of the "global" and the "local." Understood this way, globalization is accompanied by regionalization tendencies and an appraisal of local culture/customs/norms. The results and processes related to interdependency and barter between the global and the regional/local is described as "glocalization" (Robertson 1998). The re-discovery of local customs can be both an anchor and an antipode to a potentially "frightening" globalized world or a fully incorporated aspect of globalization and modernization when regional peculiarities are (successfully) put on the (global) market. Hence, glocalization does not necessarily cause conflict, but it is related to divergence and differences.

Thus, divergence theory assumes that (cultural) distinction remains and (new) tendencies towards regionalization hinder convergence as a consequence of modernization despite globalization as the leitmotiv of global development (Schneider, Naderi & Ruppenthal 2012). According to this approach, German reunification would potentially strengthen east-west differences where they existed, especially as demography-relevant behavior is often deeply rooted in customs, societal norms and culture.

1.1.3   Hybridization theory

The assumption of convergence as a consequence of globalization comes from an essentially economic perspective in which shared values, norms, culture, etc. will change according to the impulses given by the economy. Divergence theory, however, puts the emphasis on culture as an especially resilient structure, withstanding leveling and egalitarianism even though immense innovations have been adopted. Due to their holistic concept of "culture," the two theories are incompatible: either different cultures coexist or one culture is taken over and replaced by the other (Schwinn 2006).

The two competing theories heighten the argument over culture in a more or less dogmatic way. They both also discuss the role of culture but do not parameterize this essential aspect and look into culture as a concept.

There is evidence that cultures are far from being inflexible and clearly distinguished by sharp and hermetic boundaries from one culture to another. Instead, interaction, exchange and adaption between cultures are a common if not chief principle pattern from a contemporary as well as from an historical and evolutionary perspective. Cultures are neither homogeneous nor unambiguously definable. Thus, such an understanding of culture is false and even dangerous if put in a normative context, as Welsch (2000) points out. Instead, societies and their individuals are "transcultural" and shaped by hybrid tendencies.

This means that new cultures and norms that accompany modernization and globalization can be fully adopted or incorporated into the existing, local culture by partial adoption and/or reinterpretation. Even the U.S. culture (leitmotiv of globalization according to scholars promoting convergence theory) is not homogenous at all, but contains an impressive variety of (also regionally shaped) interpretations.

Thus, globalization leads to hybridization with both tendencies of convergence and divergence. Transfer, blending and interaction in cultural and structural terms does finally result in greater diversity rather than total leveling. Hybridization is potentially asymmetrical and some of the intruding elements may prove more dominant than others. Furthermore, new trends and factors can emerge in the course of hybridization that do not imperatively have direct reference to their respective origins (Schneider, Naderi & Ruppenthal 2012). In retrospect, hybridization theory is an adequate concept for assessing at least the societal and demographic aspects in the aftermath of German reunification.

1.2   Assessing the demographics of reunification on different layers and scales

Localizing Germany's reunification demographics in the hybridization theory is based on the assumption of interdependencies on two scalar levels. First, both of the distinct macro-regions, the Alte Länder and the Neue Länder, are embedded in and affected by "general" modernization and globalization, but this impulse is anticipated by different traditions and structures. Hence, it is not unlikely that the outcome of specific adaptation and interpretation are different in both regions. Indeed, given the importance of emphasized regionalism in Germany, even a broader variety than the bold east-west distinction is likely. Second, institutions, regulations and legal norms of the Federal Republic of Germany have been imposed in the Neue Länder, creating a crucial basis for accelerated convergence towards the Western model (Schneider, Naderi & Ruppenthal 2012). Hence, within the potentially hybrid development, a bias towards convergence of the Neue Länder with the Alte Länder should be expected.

However, the intercultural transmission of legacies from the old system to the new situation in East Germany and the possible spillover and diffusion of those GDR-rooted political and societal cultural legacies will hinder total convergence and fuel hybridization (see also Holtmann, Lee & Rademacher 2016). Furthermore, we can assume that the transcultural character of reunification may favor the above-mentioned bias, but there is also an exchange of culture in the other direction. Thus, reunification leads to changes in both macro-regions and therefore the potential for very varied outcomes is high. Thirdly, the existence of historically rooted differences in structures and customs (e.g. based on religion or urban-rural disparities) represents another factor of influence to be addressed.

The crucial question concerning all demographic analysis of reunification is whether society and culture in the Neue Länder have been so deeply affected by the GDR regime's political visions that specific values, ethics and customs outlast in all spheres that are not affected by enforced change due to new legislation and binding norms. Supplementary explanations could show whether the "Western model" proves to be the most attractive option and fully prevails or if new patterns emerge, supplied by elements of both the GDR and FRG legacies.

Given this pre-assumption of potentially hybrid paths after German reunification, the related demographic analysis is structured accordingly and takes into consideration scale, layers and a longitudinal perspective.

The study's focus is on the "classic" demographic factors of fertility, mortality and migration, which shape the size, structure, regional distribution and dynamics of the population. As a starting point, the long-term east-west dynamics are described and explained in a general way. A comprehensive, in-depth description and interpretation focuses on the period directly after reunification up until 25 years later.

The observed changes are classified in four perspectives, with German reunification as the cardinal point. We describe whether traceable mutations are

1. clearly reunification-related phenomena,
2. an indirect post-unification pattern, as a result of demographic de- and re-composition in the course of German reunification,
3. a fugitive trend, related to the dominating political and/or juridical framework and conditions,
4. a long term development, related to culture and societal norms the major trends of which can be identified for decades, even under changing political paradigms.

Certainly, a combination of effects is possible and – in our research – described if identified. This approach aims at a concise, straightforward localization of population trends and their possible links to reunification, which may also offer helpful hints concerning scenarios for the Korean future.

1.3   Method, Data and Restrictions

Our study relies mainly on quantitative demographic data issued at the spatial level of German *"Länder"* (Federal States). We provide a longitudinal perspective targeting in particular the moment of German reunification and the visible "traces" or "imprints" of this event in today's demographic structures. To do so, we rely on the expertise of the Bundesinstitut für Bevölkerungsforschung (BiB) concerning the last three decades' demographic trends, as BiB is a public research institute that regular monitors the population development and structure in Germany. Furthermore we refer to findings from scholarly research on German demographics since 1990 and to the publications and expertise of the Bundesinstitut für Bau-, Stadt- und Raumforschung (BBSR); the latter especially concerning questions of regional development. A major scholarly publication providing systematic and rather comprehensive knowledge on the east-west demographics of German reunification (*Die Bevölkerung in Ost- und Westdeutschland*) was published by Cassens, Luy and Scholz in 2009 and is another important basis for the correct interpretation of data. With regard to the GDR and Neue Länder, Siegfried Grundmann published a fundamental work on the population of *"Ostdeutschland"* in 1998, which is another extensive and reliable source for the better and correct understanding of East German demographics.

All data for longitudinal quantitative descriptive statistics in our project were issued by the Statistisches Bundesamt (destatis) located in Wiesbaden and have been mainly accessed via the GENESIS Pro databank. The Statistisches Bundesamt (destatis) is the governmental statistical office and provides the most accurate and detailed data on German demographics, which have been further processed and calculated by the BiB according to the specific focus of this study.

Furthermore, data of the BBSR INKAR databank, the Deutschland 25 survey (Gabriel et al. 2015) and relevant literature as well as informally published "grey literature" and statistical reports of the GDR were taken into consideration for the interpretation of data and non-demographic aspects of relevance.

Despite privileged access to national statistics of Germany, there are restrictions. Firstly, data protection standards in the Federal Republic of Germany are very strict. Therefore even anonymous information on individuals cannot be linked. Thus, for example, it is impossible to trace the individual behavior of East German citizens via statistical data. Secondly, not all demographic data since 1991 are available. In these cases, shorter time-spans were chosen or alternative indicators were selected and explored. Thirdly, GDR data was partially classified, not published or is not reliable. Hence, pre-unification data availability is incomplete and its quality is not always satisfactory.

The chapter on Korea is based on national statistics of the Republic of Korea and research by the Korea Institute for Health and Social Affairs. North Korea-related data has been gathered from different sources as this kind of data is sparse and not always reliable for the same reasons as described above concerning the GDR. Census data from the DPRK is available in more or less regular terms; scholarly research on demographics is sparse. One exception is the work published by Spoorenberg and Schekendiek (2012) on the DPRK's 1992 and 2008 censuses, as well as the 1992 monograph on North Korea's population by Eberstadt and Banister. Quite recently Ri and Ho (2017), scientists from Kim-Il-Sung University in Pong-Yang, contributed to scholarly research on healthy life expectancy in the DPRK based in 2008 census data. This publication is a unique example of a contribution to the international scientific community given by North Korean scholars, thus "first hand data and research."

Fully reliable data concerning the GDR is only available for basic indicators and a few other variables. Destatis provides a limited range of verified GDR information and information for after reunification. When using original GDR statistics, whether the information provided is fully reliable, incomplete or sugarcoated for propaganda reasons it depends in part on the topic. Many of the officially published GDR data on social issues and economic performance were narrowed and blurred. Hence, care must be taken when using and interpreting this kind of information and it requires some experience with regard to the norms, conventions and pitfalls of GDR statistics.

The comparative study of German reunification demographics relies on longitudinal observations, which poses another problem that needs to be taken into consideration: What time span is appropriate? Starting with October 3 or any date close to factual reunification might make sense at first glance, but given the short span of only 25 years, such a more or less arbitrary approach bears the risk of not detecting long term trends and developments that are only seemingly related to reunification or hidden by significant reunification-related exceptions (Schneider, Naderi, Ruppenthal 2012). Hence, typical tendencies might be (mis-)interpreted as dominating patterns. To address this problem appropriately, data for the chief demographic indicators has been explored using a GDR-FRG comparative perspective starting from the early 1980s if reliable data was available.

Another specific phenomenon of relevance for our longitudinal perspective is a de- and re-composition of regional populations. The population structure in the affected regions changed due to massive internal migration. For example, it is not exactly clear to what extent certain population trends may be related to the "specific behavior" of East German newcomers in West Germany.

For analyzing spatial demographic aspects of the GDR and the Neue Länder, it must be taken into consideration that the GDR's *Bezirke* (local governments) or *Kreise* (districts) do not correspond to the *Neue Bundesländer* (Figures 2 & 3). Thus, data analysis was carried out at the German Länder level after the reunification, but before 1990 the two states as a whole were compared.

This subdivision allows us to identify not only the formerly dominant west-east divide, but also shows when and if this pattern is replaced by other post-unification tendencies.

Figure 2: The German Democratic Republic and its Bezirke

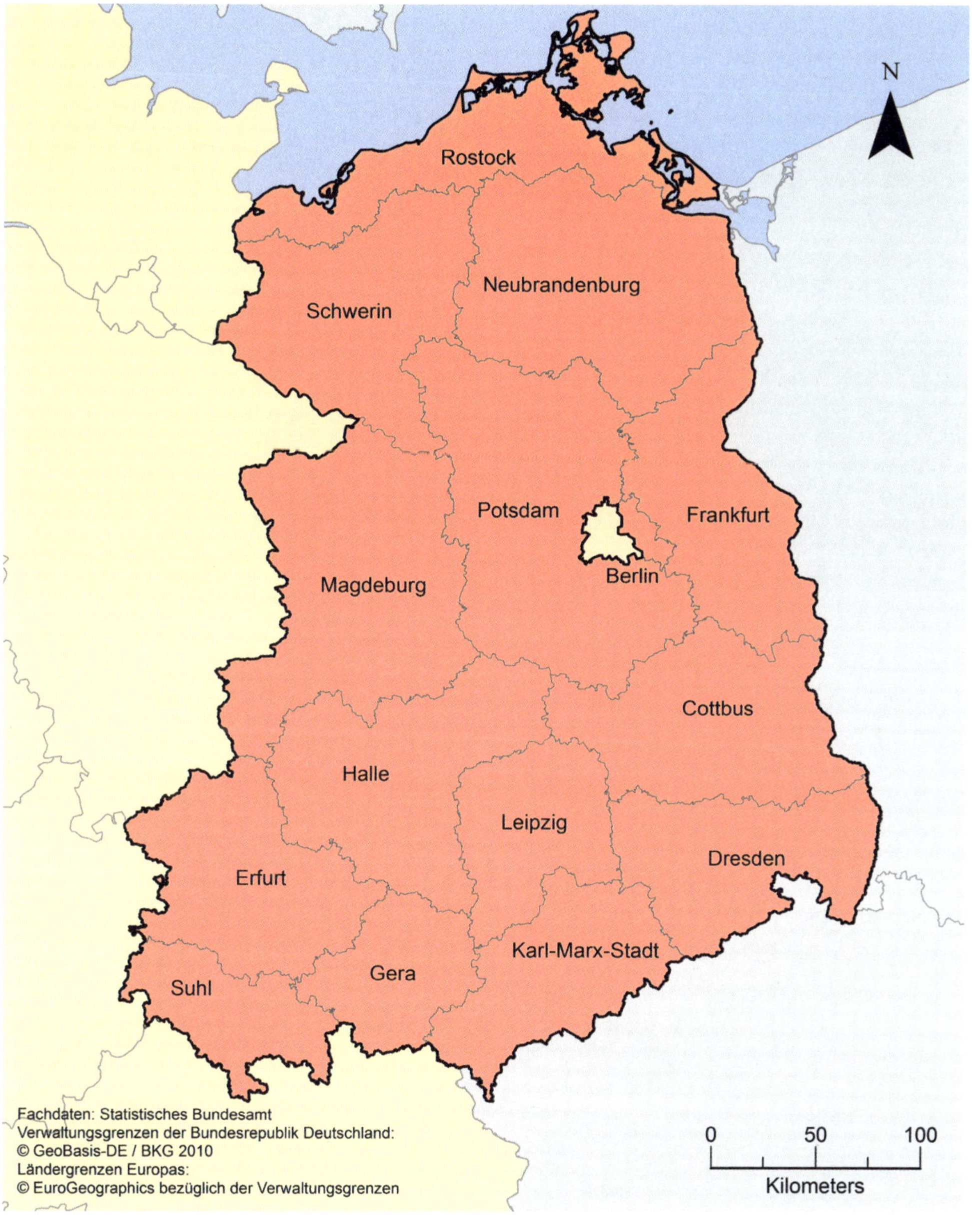

Rostock

Neubrandenburg

Schwerin

Potsdam   Frankfurt

Berlin

Magdeburg

Cottbus

Halle

Leipzig

Dresden

Erfurt

Karl-Marx-Stadt

Suhl   Gera

Fachdaten: Statistisches Bundesamt
Verwaltungsgrenzen der Bundesrepublik Deutschland:
© GeoBasis-DE / BKG 2010
Ländergrenzen Europas:
© EuroGeographics bezüglich der Verwaltungsgrenzen

0   50   100
Kilometers

Figure 3: The Neue Länder since 10/03/1990

Fachdaten: Statistisches Bundesamt
Verwaltungsgrenzen der Bundesrepublik Deutschland:
© GeoBasis-DE / BKG 2010
Ländergrenzen Europas:
© EuroGeographics bezüglich der Verwaltungsgrenzen

With regard to Berlin, it is unclear whether it "belongs" to East (Neue Länder) or West Germany (Alte Länder). In the logics of geography, Berlin is a part of East Germany. For our research, however, Berlin is partially excluded and displayed in separate tables. This is due to the fact that Berlin, as capital city, sometimes exhibits very different demographics than the other Neue Länder, which would falsify the summarized data in some cases. Furthermore, Berlin was a divided city before 1990 and statistics for the part of Berlin belonging to the FRG were certainly attributed to West Germany.

Thus, the German capital city is also special insofar as it represents German national unification on a small scale. Furthermore, due to its specific history, its small size (base effect) and its function as capital city, in many cases Berlin exhibits different trends compared to the Neue Länder. This is why particular caution must be exercised with Berlin in the context of German east-west comparisons, as explained above.

However, when the Alte and Neue Länder are compared without Berlin in a separate table, we count the capital city as a part of Neue Länder (East Germany).

The time span for our investigation of east-west differences starts in late 1990 and 1991, when unification took place. Most datasets for the Neue Länder are either incomplete or unavailable for the last three months of 1990. Between the 1991 and 2015, each year is always also regarded separately in order to identify significant demographic turnarounds and isolated, temporary trends within the years since German re-unification. The territory of the former GDR is almost equivalent to the territory of the Neue Länder – Brandenburg, Sachsen, Sachsen-Anhalt, Thüringen, Mecklenburg-Vorpommern and the capital city of Berlin. Berlin and the local municipality Amt Neuhaus (Land of Niedersachsen) are exceptions. Amt Neuhaus is a small territory of approximately 240 km² and less than 6,000 inhabitants that was formerly part of the GDR and an entity of Mecklenburg-Vorpommern until 1993. Referring to strong historic links, the Länder of Niedersachsen and Mecklenburg-Vorpommern agreed on a local government territorial reform, and municipalities that belonged to Amt Neuhaus before 1945 were re-integrated into Niedersachsen. Being of very small size, this territorial transposition does not affect the validity of data in our research.

As spatial demography is a core issue of this project, the comparison of indicators for the GDR and the Neue Länder just before and after 1990 was included in the pending deliverables. Besides the availability and reliability problems of GDR-issued data, this research is challenging as are no comparable administrative statistical territorial entities. The GDR had 15 administrative districts (14 districts and the capital city of Berlin). After reunification, these districts and Berlin were merged into five Länder. Hence, for regionalized preunification analysis and in order to facilitate the interpretation of data, the whole of GDR and FRG are discussed. The subdivision into the individual Länder becomes relevant for post-unification trends and is not systematically presented with the exception of indicators with significant regional variation.

2 Forming demographic processes of reunified Germany: Patterns of fertility, mortality and migration

German reunification furthered virtually every field of the humanities, economic and social science research on East German transformation. This great interest lasted for about a decade. This is true not only for the above-mentioned fields of research but population studies, as well. However, the longitudinal perspective is especially relevant in demography. Therefore, the demographic development of reunified Germany seen from an east-west perspective is relatively well researched. Major synopses of the Neue Länder's demography with partial reference to the macro-regional perspective of "East" and "West" include the book *Familie und private Lebensführung in West- und Ostdeutschland* (Schneider 1994) and the anthology *Die Bevölkerung in Ost- und Westdeutschland*, published in 2009 for the 20-year anniversary of German reunification in 2010 (Cassens et al. 2009). These publications represent an important basis for this study with regard to findings and interpretations of east-west demographics since 1990. Population studies maintained a steady interest in the Neue Länder-Alte Länder dichotomy, thus we can continue our observations by building upon this basis and adding knowledge from the (few) recent publications explicitly devoted to this topic.

Germany as a nation state is rather young. Indeed, the German nation was only founded in 1871 as the "German Empire" after the Franco-Prussian War (1870/71) through the union of German (speaking) principalities and kingdoms. Thus, from an historical demographic perspective, the major population trends of Germany are quite easy to reconstruct. For our undertaking of a unification-focused study, to better understand the regional West- and East-German variations before and after reunification, it is essential to outline the long-term trends in population development.

In 2015, about 82 million people were living in Germany. The population distribution and urban system is shaped by historic spatial entities as well as by the economic cores and clusters that developed since the late 19th century. As a consequence, almost exactly half of the German people live in the three western and southern German Länder of Nordrhein-Westfalen, Bayern and Baden-Württemberg. In contrast, roughly 16 million people reside in the five Neue Länder and Berlin.

The post-unification population development of Germany reveals a very distinct and easily described pattern: the Alte Länder tend to experience population growth while the Neue Länder are characterized by demographic decline (Table 1). As Germany has below replacement level fertility in all regions, population growth is based on immigration.

Table 1: Relative population changes in the Alte Länder and Neue Länder

	1991-2000	2000-2015	1991-2015
FRG/Alte Länder	4.3%	1.6%	6.0%
GDR/Neue Länder	-4.5%	-9.0%	-13.2%
Berlin	-1.9%	4.8%	2.2%
Germany	2.5%	-0.1%	2.4%

Source: Statistisches Bundesamt 2017

Figure 4: Relative change of population in German Länder 1991-2015

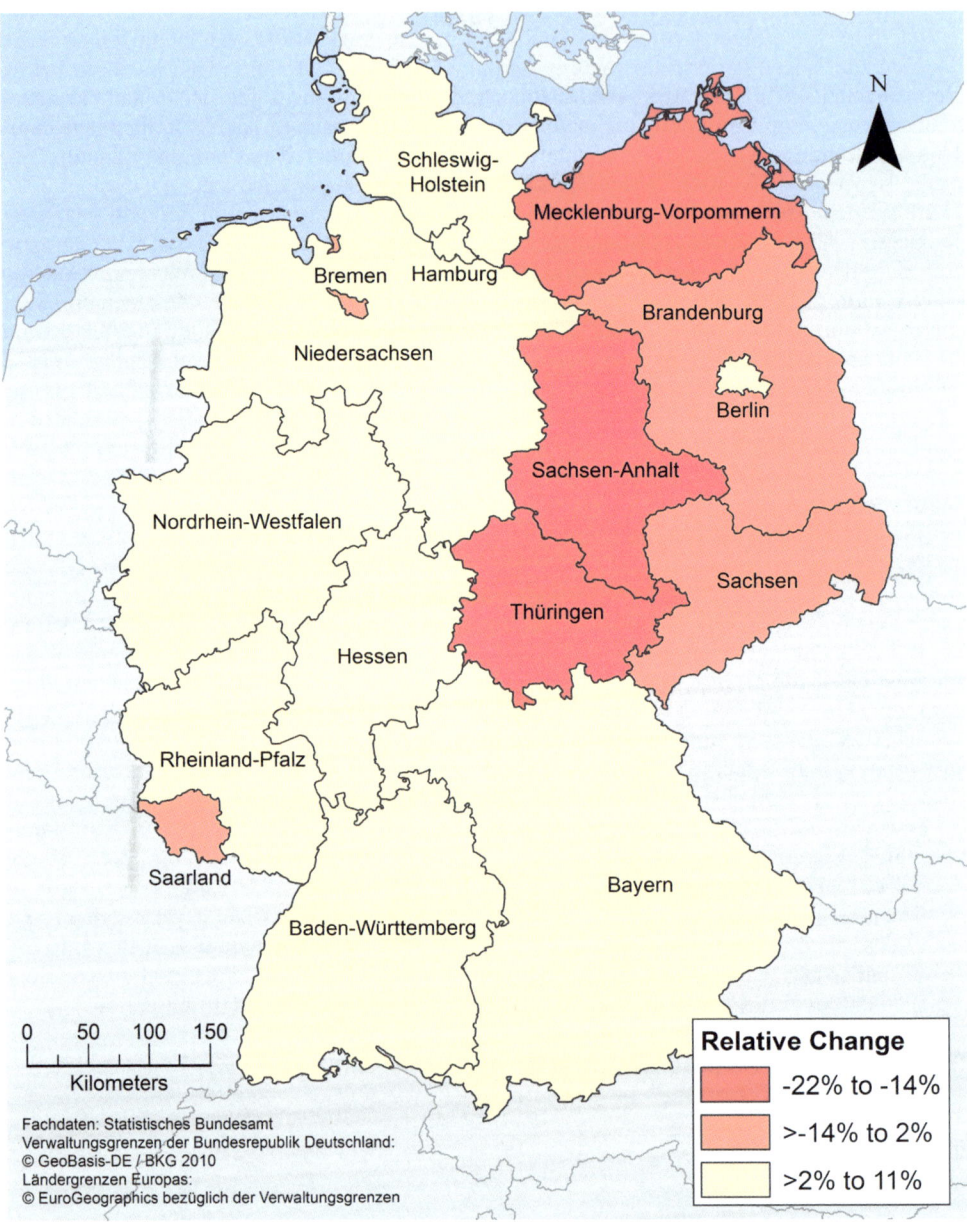

From 1991 until 2015, the population of all Neue Länder decreased or stagnated (Figure 4, Table 2). In the west, the Länder of Nordrhein-Westfalen and Saarland – both of which are characterized by old industry and structural change – experienced low dynamics in population development, but not such high losses as the Neue Länder (with the exception of Brandenburg and Berlin). Berlin and Brandenburg diverge from the "East German pattern" in that both experienced periods of population gain since 1991, while the other Neue Länder experienced continuous decline. As the TFR for all German Länder has been below replacement level for decades, stabilization and partial increases for Berlin and Branden-burg are based on immigration, as mentioned above. The main engine is Berlin as the capi-tal city attracting domestic and international immigrants. Brandenburg's figures are strongly influenced by being a virtual suburb of Berlin.

The 40 years of the GDR's existence from 1949 until 1989 are not particularly striking compared to the German population since 1841 as observed by looking at births, deaths and growth or decline in the German population in a longer time span within the area of today's state territory (Figure 5). This is due to the relatively small size of the GDR's population in comparison to the total number of people living in the Federal Republic of Germany and initial parallel trends in fertility and mortality decline until the early 1970s, as outlined in the following chapters.

Figure 5: Natural population balance on the territory of modern Germany since 1841

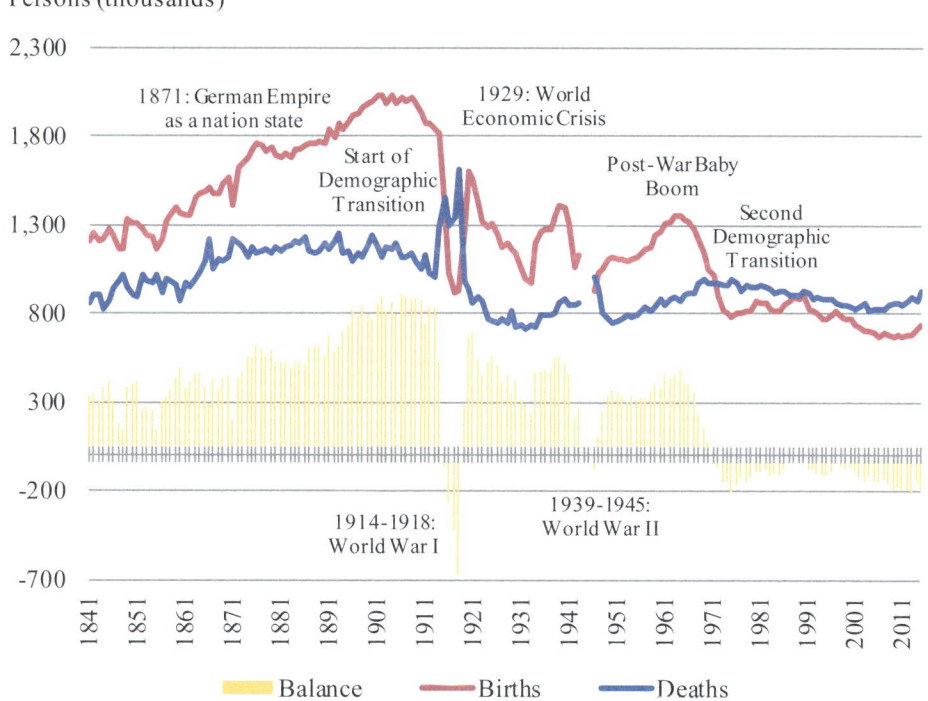

Source: Statistisches Bundesamt 2017

Therefore, the pan-German population trends over a long-term time span illustrate the shift from a pre-modern to a post-modern demographic regime as described by the theories of Demographic Transition and Second Demographic Transition (Van de Kaa 1987), deformed by demographic breaks caused by World War I, the World Economic Crisis and World War II (Figure 5).

An exclusive reflection of the GDR's population exhibits constant decline with a slight plateau in the 1980s (Figure 6). The post-war era in the GDR exhibits a similar surplus of women as the FRG and the other European countries directly affected by World War II. The continuous decrease in population size is a quite unique phenomenon for an industrialized country. In 1989, the GDR had about 2 million citizens less than in 1950. This decline and stagnation was caused by declining birth rates and the fact that the GDR did not receive significant immigration flows until contracted workers from Vietnam and Mozambique began to be recruited in the mid-1980s. In 1989, the number of foreigners living in GDR was 191,190 persons (Sozialstatistik 1990; Statistisches Amt der DDR).

Figure 6: Population of the GDR 1950 to 1989

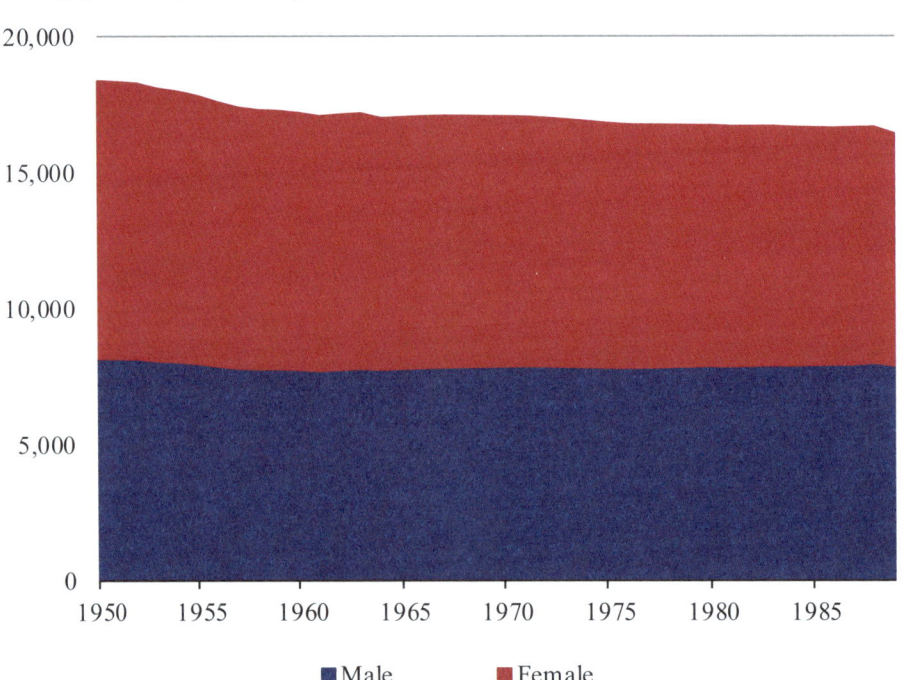

Total population (thousands)

Source: Statistisches Bundesamt 2017

Hence, because emigration was forcibly denied its citizens and due to low immigration rates, the GDR's size of population was mainly bound to the natural population balance. Actually, the GDR was an emigration shaped country or "Abwanderungsland" (Geißler 2006, S. 43).

Internal migration explains population gains and losses on a regional scale within the country. In this respect, uneven trends shaped the demographic landscape. The south of the GDR (mainly today's Sachsen and Thüringen), the former industrial heartland of East Germany, which was relatively big and dense in population, experienced losses (Eckart 1989). The capital city of Berlin and specific places in the north and east of the nation, however, became demographic growth regions. The East German state-directed economy aimed at developing peripheral places through ambitious industrialization projects . In the course of those measures, internal migration periodically focused on these respective locations. Besides that, Berlin remained a major hub for internal migration in the GDR (Freitag et. al. 1989).

As a result, on the eve of reunification, the northern part of East Germany, Berlin and a few distinct young industrial cities experienced demographic growth and shared a relatively young population. This situation rapidly changed soon after the border to West Germany was opened. Major discontinuities in former trends and patterns could be observed almost immediately with German reunification. Fertility and migration proved to show distinct post-unification patterns, which were especially accentuated in the 1990s, before becoming convergent with a pan-German trend. However, even though the main demographic drivers tend to display convergence, a variety of relevant factors for population development and structure are still different in the Alte and Neue Länder.

Regional population development on Länder level started to change rapidly due to a harsh decline in East German TFR far below replacement level and immediate east-west internal migration flows starting with the opening of the inner-German border in November of 1989 (Table 2).

Table 2: Population size of German Länder 1991, 2000, 2015

	1991		2000		2015
Baden-Württemberg	10,001,840	↗	10,524,415	↗	10,879,618
Bayern	11,595,970	↗	12,230,255	↗	12,843,514
Bremen	683,684	↘	660,225	↗	671,489
Hamburg	1,668,757	↗	1,715,392	↗	1,787,408
Hessen	5,837,330	↗	6,068,129	↗	6,176,172
Niedersachsen	7,475,790	↗	7,926,193	↗	7,926,599
Nordrhein-Westfalen	17,509,866	↗	18,009,865	↘	17,865,516
Rheinland-Pfalz	3,821,235	↗	4,034,557	↗	4,052,803
Saarland	1,076,879	↘	1,068,703	↘	995,597
Schleswig-Holstein	2,648,532	↗	2,789,761	↗	2,858,714
Berlin	3,446,031	↘	3,382,169	↗	3,520,031
Brandenburg	2,542,723	↗	2,601,962	↘	2,484,826
Mecklenburg-Vorpommern	1,891,657	↘	1,775,703	↘	1,612,362
Sachsen	4,678,877	↘	4,425,581	↘	4,084,851
Sachsen-Anhalt	2,823,324	↘	2,615,375	↘	2,245,470
Thüringen	2,572,069	↘	2,431,255	↘	2,170,714

Source: Statistisches Bundesamt 2017

The time after German unification was marked by population decline in all Neue Länder with exception of Brandenburg and Berlin, where phases of stabilization and growth were triggered by a positive balance in internal migration. Meanwhile, the Alte Länder experienced growth with only few exceptions, such as the Saarland, a relatively small Land with a problematic economic structure. Although low replacement fertility is a phenomenon for all of Germany, the gains from international and internal migration led to an increase of the population in the west, especially in economically successful regions.

Thus, in terms of general population trends, there is a clear east-west divide with 6 percent growth in the Alte Länder since 1991 and a decline in -13 percent in the Neue Länder for the same period. This significant decline in East Germany is caused by both emigration and low fertility, as will be explained in detail in the following chapters.

About 20 years after the fall of the Iron Curtain, the above-described east-west discrepancies in natural balance and migration have partially or even totally vanished. Nonetheless, the population structures within German regions differ significantly, as they were shaped by significant and sometimes long-lasting specific conditions in demographic development.

2.1 Fertility, living arrangements and related aspects

The existence of the GDR as a nation state coincides with the period of strong fertility decline, commonly described as Second Demographic Transition in western societies (van de Kaa 1987). Initially, the GDR also experienced a phase of below replacement fertility, before measures were taken to increase the number of births. In this context, a comparison of the TFR in the Federal Republic of Germany and the GDR and later the Alte Länder and Neue Länder, not only illustrates a decrease in the TFR as a consequence of unification, but provides an insight on the differences in fertility levels in political systems, with the GDR serving as an example of a state with pronatalistic politics as a reaction to fertility decline.

2.1.1 Total Fertility Rate and Cohort Fertility

Comparing both entities in terms of changes in TFR, the post-war era exhibits a rapid increase in all of Germany with an even higher TFR in the GDR compared to the Federal Republic during the first years after the founding of the two states (Figure 7). This variance is related to post-war demographic imbalances related to the variably difficult living conditions in German regions and flows of migration, including refugees from former German territories (namely Eastern Prussia and Silesia). This difference in fertility was soon leveled out between both states, firstly due to a similar "pan-German" fertility pattern and the fact that a significant number of young GDR citizens (just those generations that caused the higher TFR perviously) fled the country towards the Federal Republic of Germany. This massive loss of population due to out-migration to the west was one chief reason for the hermetic closure of the border by the GDR in 1961.

Figure 7:   The total fertility rate (TFR) of GDR/Neue Länder and FRG/Alte Länder from 1949 to 2015

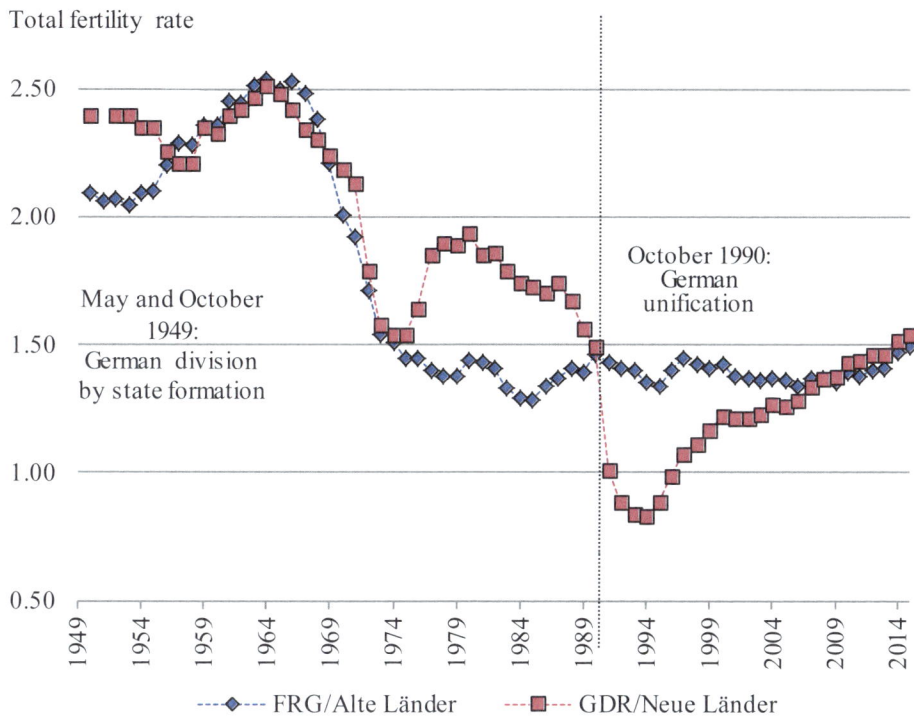

Source: Statistisches Bundesamt 2017

From 1955 onwards, when the major period of post-war reconstruction in both German states was in full blossom, until the early 1970s, the TFR of the Federal Republic of Germany and GDR was very high and very similar in both parts of Germany. The period from the 1950s to the 1960s has been called the baby boom era, where almost everybody married and marriage and children were almost universally linked (Dorbritz 2008). After a continuous increase, the TFR rapidly declined from around 2.5 to 1.5 within 12 years from 1963 to 1975. As for West Germany and partially also for the GDR, this phenomenon can be explained with the hypothesis of the Second Demographic Transition, as mentioned above. Furthermore, in East Germany, in addition to the general tendencies towards individualization (even within the very structured socialist society), a significant lack of lodgings (for young couples) and the systematic increase in women's employment due to socialist political and economic doctrine contributed to low fertility.

For the Federal Republic of Germany, the TFR settled at a low level between 1.3 and 1.5 with minor amplitudes down and up. In a long-term perspective, the TFR of the west remains at a low but very stable level.

This is not the case for the GDR and Neue Länder after 1990, where the TFR showed high amplitudes within 30 years. For a long time, low fertility was not seen as problem in the Federal Republic of Germany, as the surplus in mortality was easily outmatched and overbalanced by international immigration. Thus, population decline was not an issue. The GDR by contrast did not receive any significant immigration and was de facto a potential "out-migration" state, which put enormous effort into hindering its citizens by force from leaving the country. This also means that the population size and demographic structure of the GDR was fully dependent on births. Therefore the regime successively focused on population and family policy, especially as until the closure of the border, the 1950s emigration of mainly young people affected the population structure and made it important to a) maintain a level of fertility above or around replacement level and b) ensure a high degree of female labor-force participation.

Thus, the GDR government was sensitive to demographic issues and reacted almost immediately to below-replacement-level fertility. In 1976, the party convention of the socialist party SED (Sozialistische Einheitspartei Deutschlands) resolved a significant intensification of family-related, pro-natalistic measures. These included financial and workplace-related incentives for women and families (e.g. time off) as well as – and this is a triggering aspect – the expansion of family and child-related infrastructure such as nurseries, after school-care and preferential assignment of housing to couples with children, the latter a very attractive stimulus in a society with a notorious lack of dwellings.

As a consequence, the TFR subsequently started climbing and almost reached replacement level in the late 1970s. This phenomenon is remarkable also insofar as in the same period, in 1971, voluntary abortion was introduced/legalized as a measure of empowerment of women. This factor, in combination with the large availability of contraceptives, makes the rise of the TFR an unexpected development. The increased TFR is commonly interpreted as a success of the pro-natalistic policy with true freedom of choice for women. This is partially true, but before unification the birth rate decreased again as fast as it had climbed about 10 years before. Thus the impressive variation of the TFR needs to be backed up with additional birth-related statistics. Indeed, some of the TFR dynamics in the mid-1970s were due to the methodological weakness of the indicator itself. The TFR is not an exact value, but a proxy for the reproductive behavior of all women of childbearing potential, based on real births observed during a given period of time. Hence, the TFR offers orientation but is not fully reliable if there is a change of fertility patterns in process. Postponements of childbirth lead to an underestimation and successively earlier childbirths to an overestimation of fertility.

In the GDR, also triggered by family-friendly social policy, the average age of women giving birth declined between 1960 and 1976 and remained rather stable until 1987. West Germany experienced a gradual increase of that age from 1981 onwards.

One very reliable indicator to describe fertility patterns over time is cohort fertility, the final number of children, which is available only for birth cohorts who have finished their reproductive period (currently for the birth cohorts from 1935 until 1970 (Figure 8). These cohorts cover basically all of the relevant female population that could have given birth to children during the GDR era. This reveals that fertility in the GDR was generally higher than in the Federal Republic of Germany, but the difference between both nations was not nearly as distinctive as the TFR would suggest. Hence it is by large a statistical artifact due to the methodological weakness of the TFR as an indicator that the GDR was (wrongly) estimated to be so much more prolific than the Federal Republic of Germany, which is also underlined if the net reproduction rate is examined. However, for contemporary analysis, the TFR remains the only available indicator.

Figure 8: Cohort fertility of women born 1935 to 1970

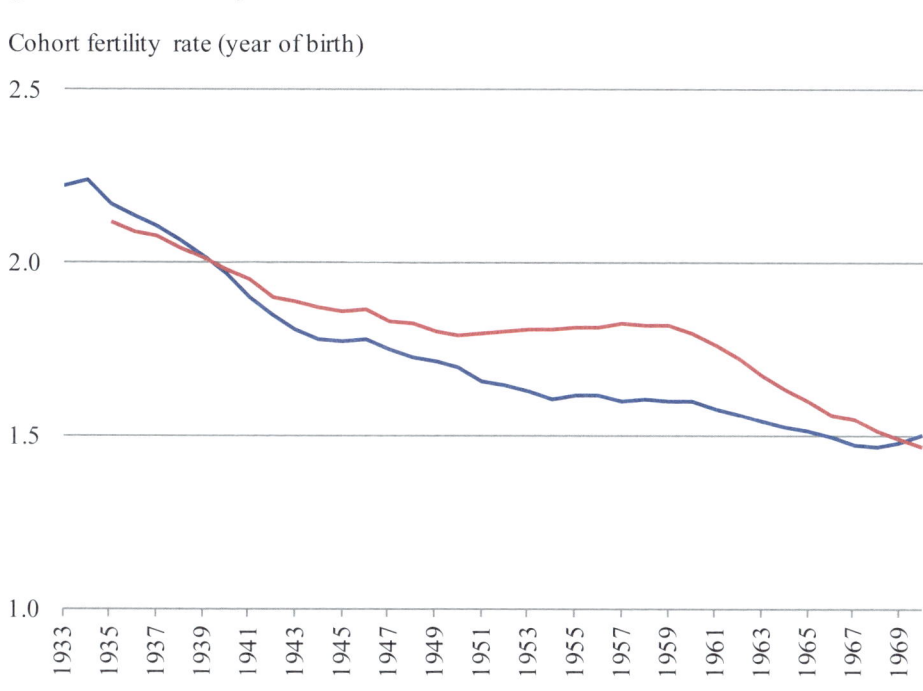

Cohort fertility rate (year of birth)

Source: Statistisches Bundesamt 2017

Given the higher fertility in GDR, a closer look at the post-unification dynamics of East Germany is especially interesting. As a consequence of the regime change, the TFR of the GDR/Neue Länder dropped to an extremely low level from 1.5 in 1990 to 0.83 in 1994.

Considering the higher TFR before unification, it is a remarkable phenomenon and with the exception of the Länder Mecklenburg-Vorpommern and Berlin, the TFR in 1991 was even below 1 for Brandenburg, Sachsen-Anhalt, Thüringen and Sachsen (Figure 9).

Low fertility in times of crisis and uncertainty is not an unknown phenomenon in historic demography. In the context of the world economic crisis in the late 1920s, a decrease in fertility was experienced in all affected countries, including Germany. As for the post-unification shock, it is quite plausible that decisions about having a child were postponed by many couples in order to first anticipate the regime change and be re-assured of their respective individual positions and perspectives in reunified Germany before starting (or continuing) a family. The favorable conditions for young mothers from the former GDR fell away (including a secure workplace, generous family support and comprehensive childcare). Together with a difficult labor market, the role model of a working mother was much more difficult to maintain for women in the Neue Länder.

Yet, this "transformation shock" may explain the harsh decline in fertility for a period of about two to three years. A relatively rapid increase in fertility towards preunification patterns would have been expected after a time for individual orientation. This rapid restoration did not ensue, but the TFR in the Neue Länder remained extremely low for another two years before climbing slowly towards the pan-German average of about 1.3 to 1.4 in 2015 (Figure 10).

Figure 9: Total Fertility Rate in German Länder 1991

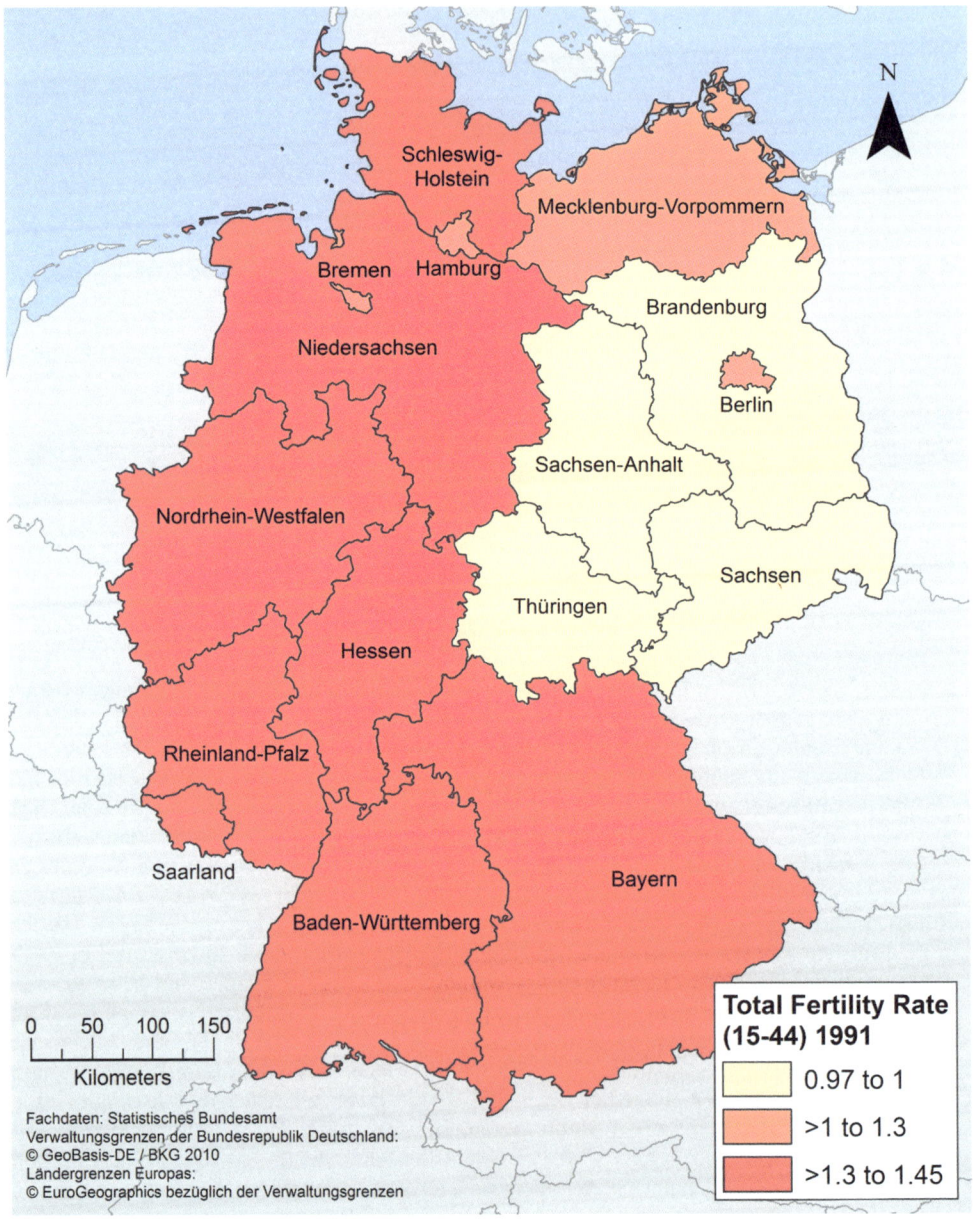

Figure 10: Total Fertility Rate in German Länder 2015

The rather long period of extremely low fertility in the Neue Länder is based on two major factors. The first was the above-mentioned phase of post-unification related to individual uncertainty and a "wait and see attitude." The second was that the lifestyle and consumer patterns of young East Germans adapted very quickly to the "western" lifestyle. In the Neue Länder, the average age of married women upon giving birth to their first child was 25 years in 1991. In the Alte Länder it was 27 years (Conrad et al. 1996). Still, the age of first birth remained earlier in the east than in the west, thus there are still distinctive differences despite a convergence of the TFR (Goldstein & Kreyenfeld 2011).

With the rapid adoption of "western-style" postponement of births in the Neue Länder, the TFR remained at an extreme low for half a decade. Massive east-west migration in the first years after reunification, namely by young people, additionally lowered the birth rate: the "potential East German mothers" were in West Germany and gave birth to their children there (Figure 11).

25 years after reunification, the above-described long-term divergence in fertility from the high TFR-related GDR era to the low fertility post-unification phase has become a full convergence. In 2015, the TFR is even slightly higher in the Neue Länder than in the rest of the nation (Figures 8 & 10).

Figure 11: Mothers' mean age at first childbirth in existing marriages in East and West
Germany 1960 to 2015

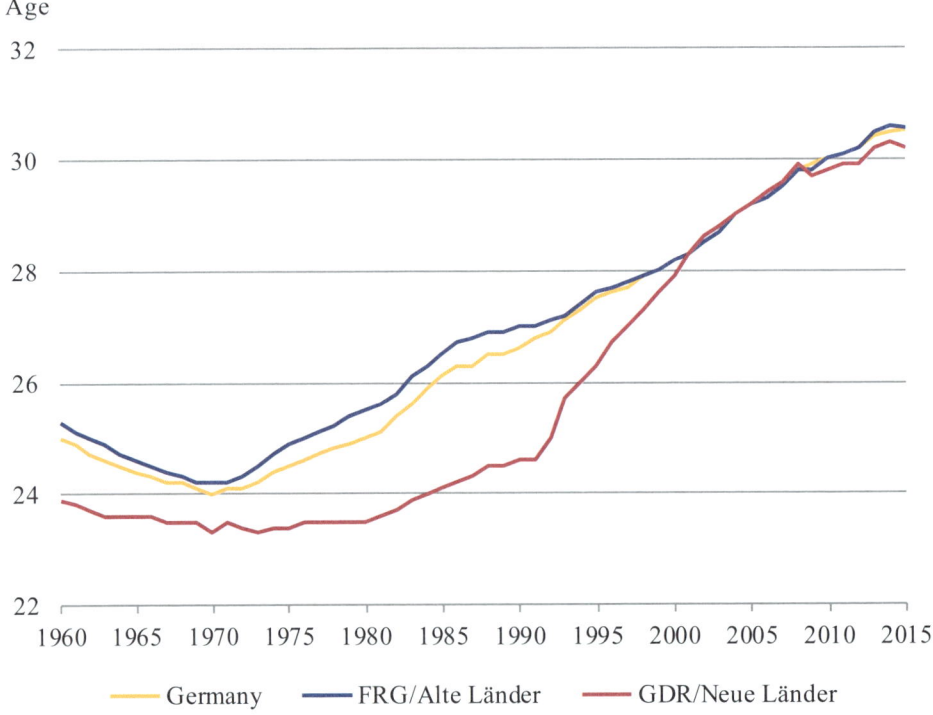

Source: Statistisches Bundesamt 2017

2.1.2   Fertility decline and children per women in the light of the CTFR

Observing the development of the TFR in all German Länder since 1991, a sequence of decline and increase can be identified for the first 15 years after reunification. The last 10 years, however, were a decade of a constant (but very low) increase in fertility. While the low TFR in 1991 for the Neue Länder is a consequence of reunification, the general trend in TFR tendencies is rather convergent for most German regions. The current increase in the TFR is partially related to the realization of postponed childbirth, thus another increase in the average age of mothers at the birth of their first child.

However, fertility is at a low level in all German Länder. For the Alte Länder, this low level was achieved for the first time in the early 1970s and remained basically at this level for more than 40 years with no significant variation. In 2015, fertility is fully convergent all over also with only minor variations. It is very unlikely that this pattern will change in the near future. That said, we must note that Germany has been experiencing a slight increase in TFR since 2013. However, it still remains unclear whether this gain is based on changing behavior or a statistical effect (e.g., tempo effect).

So what are the main reasons for today's Germany remaining far below replacement fertility? Despite the fact that the TFR all over Germany is similar, there is a slight west-east divide in the reasons for low fertility and childlessness. In the Alte Länder two factors are mainly relevant. First, a predominating "traditional," conservative understanding of "good" parent- and motherhood exhibits considerable persistence, even among young adults (Diabaté 2015). This means that after having given birth to a child, "good" mothers should stay at home or suspend professional life (if they have not been housewives already) for at least three (the age when children in Germany traditionally can be sent to a kindergarten) and up to six years (the age when children start going to elementary school). In this context, conception, maternity and marriage are still much more tied together than in Eastern Germany. To fulfill the high expectations related to this kind of "good," comprehensive motherhood, the single child or two-child family became a predominating phenomenon.

The other West German phenomenon linked to this understanding of motherhood is willful intended childlessness. This phenomenon is especially common among highly educated and career-oriented women (Bujard 2015). A significant number of couples in the Alte Länder deem the combination of both career and motherhood incompatible (Bujard & Dorbritz 2015). Professional day care is not always regarded as an equivalent to childcare by the mother and the day care infrastructure in the Alte Länder is (still) limited, especially in terms of quantity (availability of places). These factors favor childlessness or low fertility in the western part of Germany.

As a consequence of pro-natalistic politics of the GDR and a well developed daycare infrastructure going hand in hand with social acceptance (and even expectations) of women's employment, the situation is quite different in the Neue Länder. Therefore, childlessness is less frequent in the Neue Länder than in the Alte Länder.

However the low total number of children in families with children is similar in all regions of the country. In the Neue Länder, socio-economic factors relate to low fertility. Fixed-term work contracts, low salaries and general economic uncertainty hinder people from having large families. On the other hand, it should not be forgotten (with reference to cohort fertility in FRG and GDR) that large families with three or more children decreased in both countries a long time before reunification (Bujard & Sulak 2016). The latter becomes obvious when the Cohort Total Fertility Rate (CTFR) for the birth cohorts 1933 to 1968 is examined in depth (Figures 12 & 13).

Figure 12: Decomposition of the second birth decline (cohort total fertility rate (CTFR) 1933-68) - Western Germany

Effects of the components on CTFR change to cohort 1933

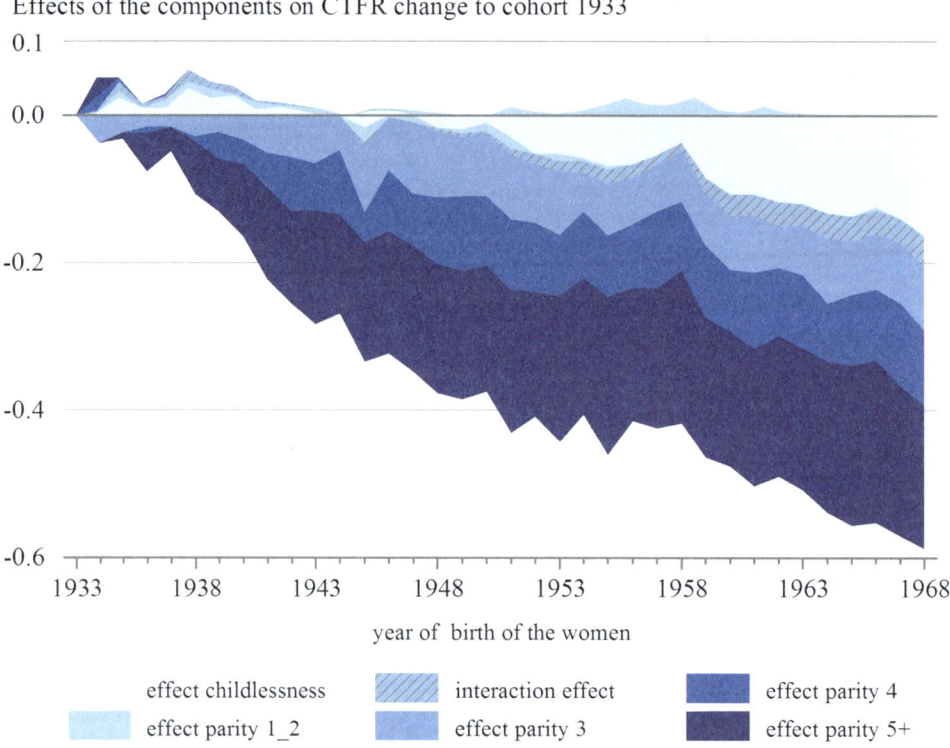

year of birth of the women

effect childlessness	interaction effect	effect parity 4
effect parity 1_2	effect parity 3	effect parity 5+

Source: Own design based on Bujard/Sulak 2016

The general decline in the CTFR can be divided into four components: increasing childlessness, decreasing shares of higher order births (3+), a combined (interaction) effect and a changing ratio of first and second births.

In Western Germany, this decrease for the cohorts of 1933 and 1947 is solely based on the decline in women with three or more children. Since the cohort of 1947, two-thirds of the CTFR decline has been caused by increasing childlessness. In Eastern Germany, the CTFR decline between the cohorts of 1933 and 1944 is mostly based on the decline in women with three or more children. For women born between 1945 and 1959, the CTFR remains at a stable level in particular because of a positive effect of the ratio of first and second births. Only since the cohort of 1960, did childlessness also play a decisive role in Eastern Germany.

Hence, low fertility in the Alte as well as the Neue Länder can also be seen to some extent as a path-dependent, long-term, dominant, convergent phenomenon connected to the second demographic transition with smaller families and childlessness as triggers.

Figure 13: Decomposition of the second birth decline (cohort total fertility rate (CTFR) 1933-68) - Eastern Germany

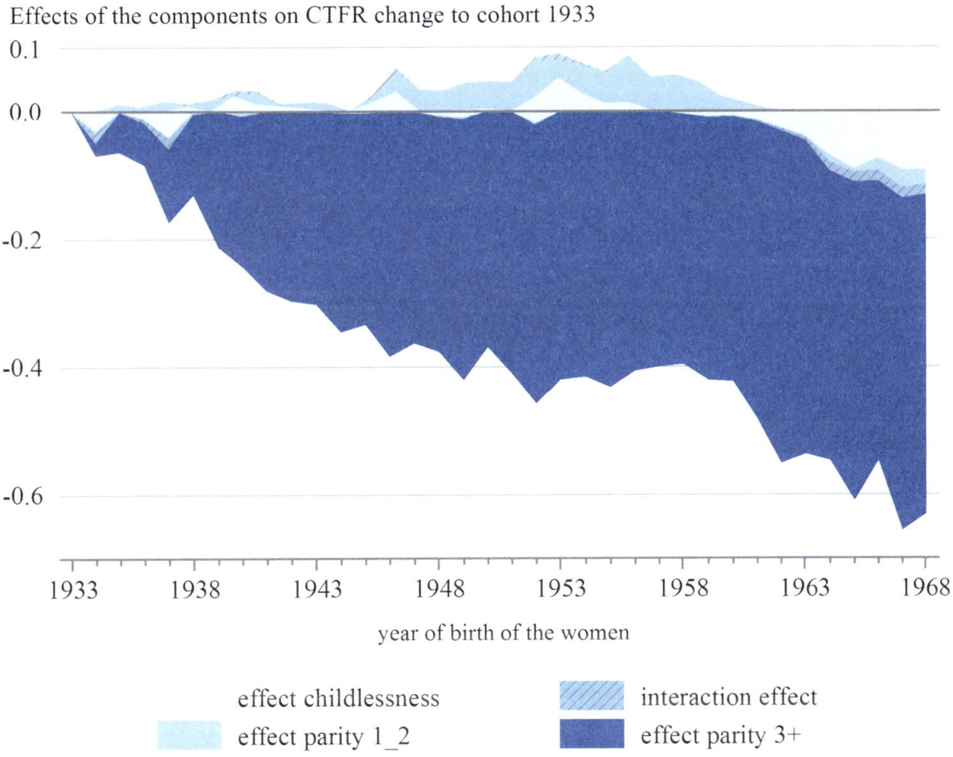
Effects of the components on CTFR change to cohort 1933
0.1
0.0
-0.2
-0.4
-0.6
1933
1938
1943
1948
1953
1958
1963
1968
year of birth of the women
effect childlessness
effect parity 1_2
interaction effect
effect parity 3+

Source: Own design based on Bujard/Sulak 2016

2.1.3 Marriage and divorce

With regard to the total number of marriages, there was an iconic decline just at the moment of reunification. From this low point, however, no steep increase to "recover" the former level can be seen, but interestingly, a gradual decline in the Alte Länder's rate towards convergence with the Neue Länder in 2010 (Figure 14). Hence, for marriage, the trend is convergent and the marriage behavior in all parts of Germany has changed rapidly (Neue Länder) or gradually (Alte Länder) due to changed perceptions of marriage on the personal level.

In 1990, the age of first marriage of around 22 years was earlier in the Neue Länder than in the western part of the nation. This ratio changed in 2003/2004. Since then, people in the Neue Länder tend to marry later than in the Alte Länder.

Figure 14: Crude marriage rate 1950-2015

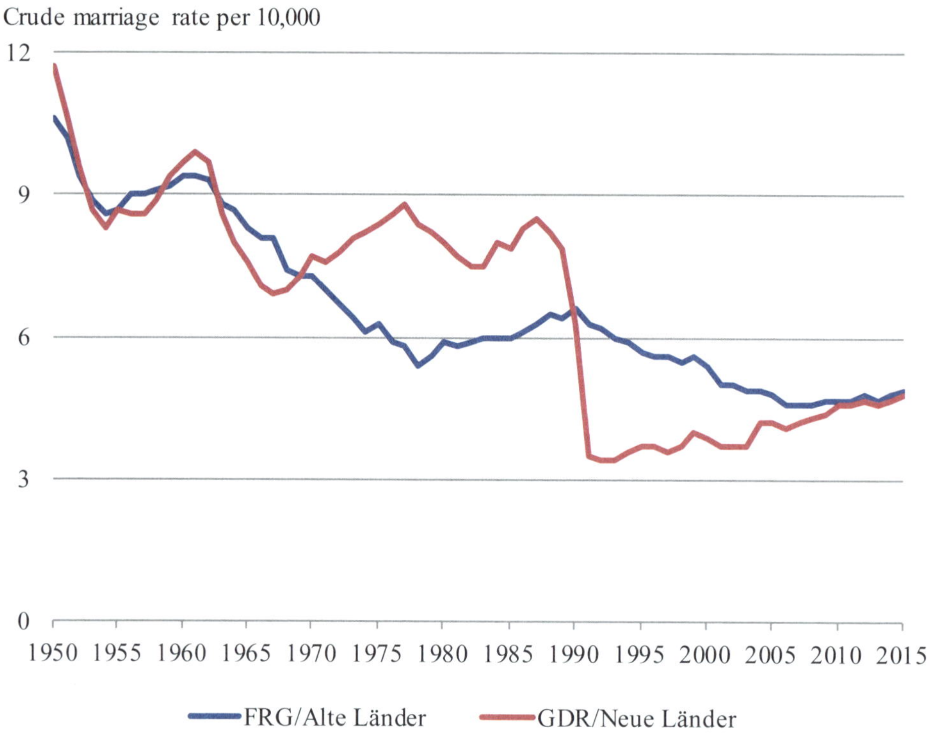

Crude marriage rate per 10,000

●━━━FRG/Alte Länder   ●━━━GDR/Neue Länder

Source: Statistisches Bundesamt 2017

Another childbirth and partnership-related difference between GDR and FRG is the number of children born to non-married parents, as described above. Changing norms, values and family patterns in German society have led to a subsequent increase of the number of children who were not born within marriage. Thus, the proportion of non-marital births has increased in all of Germany, but exhibits the highest numbers in the Neue Länder.

An important origin for this behavior can be found in the specific approach of the GDR regime towards non-married parents and single parents. Non-marital partnership in the GDR was not a mainstream phenomenon, but it was socially much more accepted than in FRG. Moreover it was legally backed, as non-married parents and single partners had the same comprehensive social benefits, including childcare from the first weeks after birth on, as married couples. Thus, the number of births outside of marriage was and remains significantly higher in the GDR and the Neue Länder (Figure 15).

In this respect, a completely different pattern, a pattern of clear east-west divergence, can be observed. The number of non-married parents used to be higher in the eastern part of Germany even before the creation of two German states. Since reunification, however, the divergence even grew. Also, in West Germany the number of unmarried couples with children gradually increases but the difference between the Alte and Neue Länder remains significant.

Figure 15: Number of children born out of wedlock 1949-2015

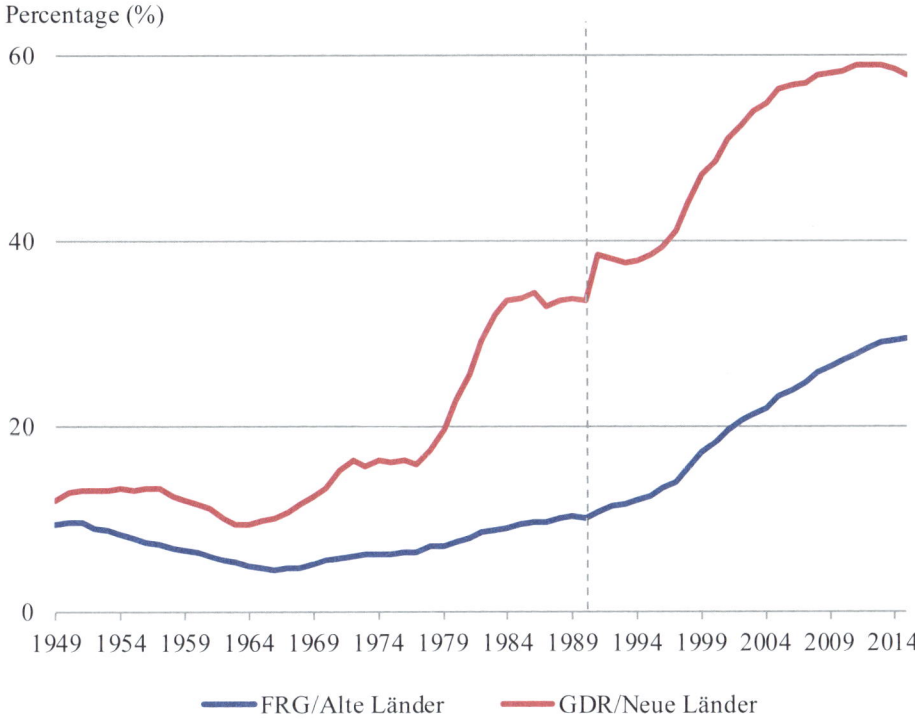

Source: Statistisches Bundesamt 2017

The larger number of non-married parents today is also due to the fact that couples in the Neue Länder tend to marry after their first child is born; a behavior that is entirely different from the behavior in the Alte Länder (Grünheid 2009). This also is concomitant with the increasing average age at first marriage: if the birth of the first child is postponed and there is a tendency to marry after childbirth, the average age at first marriage also rises.

However it would be false to read this divergent pattern as a genuine heritage of the GDR's socialist society, although its values and norms do play a major role in an explanation. Looking back further in demographic history, we can see that the proportion of children of non-married parents was higher in the territories which form the northern parts of today's Neue Länder than in other regions of Germany even long before German division (Klüsener & Goldstein 2016). The former social structure in these territories (poor peasants unable to afford marriage) and religious customs (a little more tolerance towards non-married couples by the Lutheran church, predominant in the north of Germany) are possibly the basis of this pattern, which has been maintained as a behavior under changing regimes and times until today. Hence, a long-term demographic behavior was more or less anticipated by the GDR's regime and the trend also continues in unified Germany regardless of the political framework. Also marriage itself is not necessarily the "one and dominant" living arrangement in Germany – a pluralization of patterns can be observed (Wagner & Cifuentes 2014).

Today, almost every third family in Germany does not correspond to the classic model of a married (opposite sex) couple with children. About 20 percent of mothers and fathers are single parents and 10 percent of the parents raise their children in a non-marital or same-sex life community. The proportion of married couples in families in the Neue Länder is around 50 percent, while in the Alte Länder three-quarters of parents are married. At the same time, the proportion of non-married living arrangements is highest in the Neue Länder (22%), while the lowest proportion is reported for Rheinland-Pfalz in the west (6%). All in all, marriage still remains the most common form of adults living together in Germany.

Legal framework and societal norms do shape people's behavior, but it depends on the specific aspect, how strong and how persistent its influence is. The matter of divorce in an east-west comparison is such a case where a changing frame led to changed behavior.

If we take a closer look at current divorces in the Neue and Alte Länder, it is revealed that their numbers in East Germany are lower than in the rest of the country. However, the difference is very small compared to the period just before and after reunification, when it was significant (Figure 16). The number of divorces in the GDR was about one and a half times higher than in the FRG in the 1980s.

Figure 16: Divorces per 10,000 marriages 1950-2015

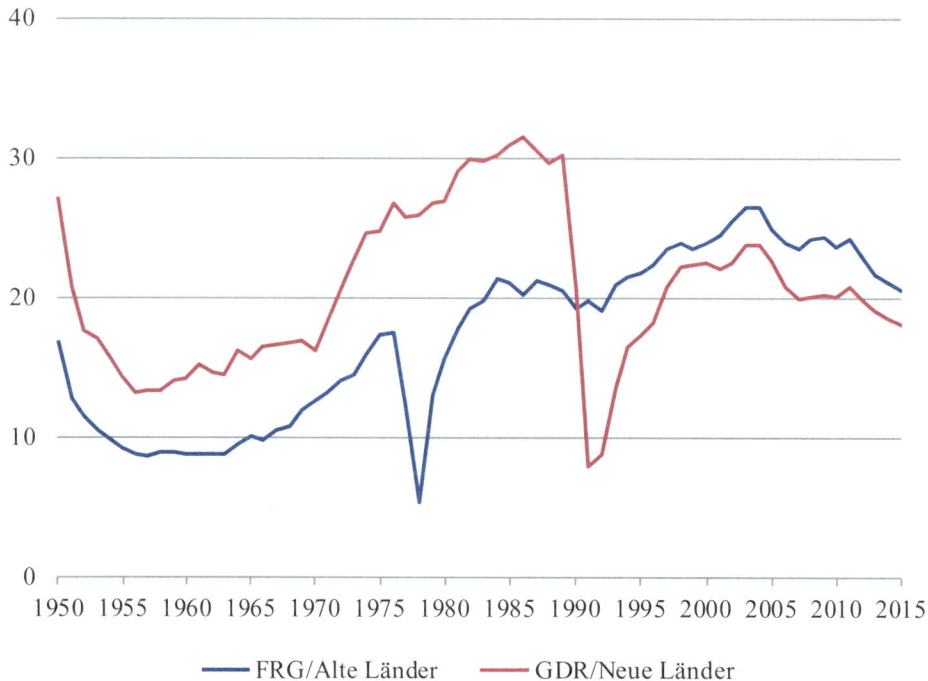

Source: Statistisches Bundesamt 2017

Actually in both states, divorce was handled and seen in a quite different way from a cultural and juridical point of view. This is also why a pan-German divorce rate before 1989 cannot be produced statistically (Grünheid 2015). Aliments after divorce were rare (unusual) in the GDR and women could always find work (there was a "right to work" guaranteed by the GDR constitution). Overall, it was much easier to divorce in the GDR than in the FRG.

With reunification in 1990, the divorce rate in the Neue Länder declined suddenly and sharply. This is explained by the fact that matters of partnership and "quality of marriage" were not individual top priorities for most individuals in the Neue Länder just after reunification. Other issues, mainly job related, were deemed more important. Furthermore, the more complicated divorce and marriage laws of the FRG were implemented. People were uncertain about financial consequences related to divorce under this new juridical framework (such as the need to hire a costly lawyer). Thus, potential "pending" divorces were postponed and divorce rates started to increase from the mid-1990s on (Grünheid 2013). Interestingly, the average divorce rate of the Alte Länder has not been reached yet, accordingly there is still a difference between the former GDR and FRG. Before reunification, this difference was distinct, with more divorces in the east. After reunification, the values held in both parts of Germany are more similar, but with lower divorce rates in the Neue Länder. This divergence remains. In general, the numbers of divorces are decreasing in Germany. This is due to several factors.

Marriage is not the predominant living arrangement of couples. Even though homosexual marriage was recently allowed, the number of expected same-sex unions will not have a notable effect (and then only for a very short time). This loss of importance of marriage is still a continuing phenomenon. Therefore, as less people get married, the potential for possible divorce (measurable in absolute numbers) is decreasing. Separations of unmarried couples remain undocumented.

However, even the relative divorce rate has been decreasing recently (Statistisches Bundesamt, Pressemitteilung Nr. 237, 11.07.2017). For West Germany, the divorce rates showed an increasing trend from the 1970s up to 2005. Explanations for more marital "stability" are that couples tend to marry later, thus the decision to marry is made when living as a couple has been "tested" for a longer time and the relationship has proven stable and durable. Hence, married (as well as unmarried) couples seem to take more effort and care for their respective partnerships.

Furthermore, it is very likely that the demographic structure of Germany is having an indirect impact on decreasing divorce rates. With an ageing society (the average age of German people in 2015 was 44.2 years, median age 46 years), the proportion of people who are at an age where they have either already divorced or are unlikely to divorce in the future is increasing. This may also be an important factor for the Neue Länder, where ageing has progressed much further than in the Alte Länder. Thus, the current low and still decreasing divorce rate in the Neue Länder is partially also related to the age structure.

However, divorce rates in reunified Germany are firstly related to the respective legal system: the liberal GDR legislation facilitated divorce, the conservative FRG laws are a hindering factor. This is displayed quite clearly by the change in divorce rates in east and west over recent decades. Furthermore, the long-term trend of changed living arrangements and lessened importance of marriage leads to fewer divorces in purely statistical terms. In the Neue Länder ageing and decomposition of the demographic structure (loss of younger population due to emigration and low birth rates) also abet low divorce rates, as a) fewer people are married (loss of potential for divorce as a formal, statistically relevant act) and b) those persons who are married are at an age where divorce is increasingly unlikely to happen. However, the described differences and changes in living arrangements between the Alte and Neue Länder as well as for Germany as whole are mainly shaped by the younger generation and are not an unambiguous consequence of reunification, but evolved over the course of "general" changes in society and culture. Thus, even convergent patterns do not imperatively prove convergence by absorption and adoption of "western" behavior by the Neue Länder's citizens, but convergence over the course of the German pathway of current modernization, which is clearly different from the pre-1990 FRG's norms and specifics, as shown above.

2.1.4 Number and composition of households

The increasing individualization of society, institutional change with decreasing significance and benefits of marriage and the increasing proportion of the older population are accompanied by a rising number of small households. There were about 40 million private households in Germany in 2015. At the time of reunification, this number was 4.7 million lower. This increase in household numbers can be observed in all German Länder, with the exception of Sachsen-Anhalt where the number stagnated.

The structure of households, however, underwent significant changes since reunification. In this respect, a clear shift from east-west divergence to convergence could be observed. The number of households with children was higher in the former GDR and the Neue Länder in 1991. Since then, the proportion of larger households, in which three and more persons live and work together, declined in favor of single and two-person households.

For all of Germany, the number of two-person households increased since reunification whereas the largest increase was recorded for one-person households. Ageing and low fertility are the main reasons for this tendency. Hence, the number of households with children is constantly declining. In 2015, the proportion of households without and with children in Germany was roughly 70 to 30, while in 1991 it was 60 to 40. However, looking at the number of children in private households, the structures have hardly changed since 1991 for Germany as a whole. In the Neue Länder, the situation is different: the proportion of households with one child rose from 51 percent to 65 percent between 1991 and 2015. At the same time, the proportion of households with two children decreased by 10 percentage points to 30 percent. In 2015, the Neue Länder had the highest share of households with only one child.

Individualization and ageing of society mean that today, the majority of people in Germany no longer live as a family in one household. The number of families in Germany declined from 9.4 million to 8.0 million between 1996 and 2015. This decline is accompanied by a rise in the number of couples without children and single people.

2.1.5   Cultural conceptions of family as a socio-demographical marker between East and West?[1]

Family life in Europe is a rather well researched topic. Explanations for changes in behavior expressed by declining birth rates, a later age at marriage or at first birth and a general increase in births out of wedlock are subject to several theoretical approaches (see also Lück, Diabaté & Ruckdeschel 2017). The probably most common idea of a second demographic transition, which assumes that industrialization has led to stable economic wealth, which in turn has caused a change in values connected to a series of changes in the orientation of family lives (van de Kaa, 1987; Lesthaeghe, 1995; Surkyn and Lesthaeghe, 2004), has already been mentioned. The theory of individualization (Beck, 1992; Beck and Beck-Gernsheim, 1993) is also often stressed in this context, as it supposes there is a push towards individualization that encourages people to develop and pursue individual life plans, leading to a pluralization of forms of living. Another approach was chosen by Becker (1993), emphasizing human capital. In today's Europe, women tend to achieve higher educational levels, which, as a consequence, increase their opportunity costs when leaving the labor market to take care of children. Thus, children and the "traditional" family are perceived more critically by this generation of women. Social welfare and infrastructure is subject to the value of children approach (Nauck and Klaus 2007, Nauck, 2005). It is presupposed that in modern societies with improved healthcare systems and care in old age, the economic, utilitarian value of children has significantly declined compared to earlier decades, thus children are of psychological, emotional value but not a necessity for individual and collective "survival." This reduction in the emotional aspect of parenting gives little incentive for large families, as one or two children can easily fill this psychological, emotional desire. However, the desire to have children and form a family has not vanished. It is actually rather stable, despite all theories explaining the decline in birth rates in developed societies (Mayer and Trommsdorff, 2010; Virtala et al., 2011). Even "traditional" forms of living together (paid work by the father and childcare by the mother) remain persistent patterns (Reher, 1998; 2004; Hakim, 2003; Fuwa, 2004; Lewis et al., 2008; Miller and Sassler, 2010). Thus, within the European context, both behaviors can be observed, often parallel in same societies.

In the Neue Länder and Alte Länder, this gap becomes obvious as well. The Leitbild survey (BiB 2012 and 2016) gives an insight into the large variety of types "beyond the nuclear family" (Widmer and Jallinoja 2008) and differences within family lives in Germany (Diabaté & Ruckdeschel 2015; Lück, Diabaté & Ruckdeschel 2017; Schneider 1994). The German word *Leitbild* is derived from the verb *leiten,* which means to lead or to guide and the noun *Bild,* meaning picture or image. Thus, in our context, a Leitbild is a "mental picture" or "guiding image" as also suggested by Pfau Effinger (2004: 382)[2]. It expresses an idea or a conception of how things in a certain context should be, work or look and it can have the character of a role model. We refer to Leitbilder as sets of collectively shared and pictured conceptions of a "normal" state or process, in the sense that these are widespread, socially

---

[1]   This chapter is based on the representative (Family) Leitbild research carried out among 20 to 39-year-old Germans by BiB since 2012 and the theoretical considerations within this project (Lück, Diabaté & Ruckdeschel 2017; Schneider, Diabaté & Ruckdeschel 2015, Lück et. al. 2013).

[2]   She defines them as "typical societal ideal representations, norms and values regarding the family and the societal integration of women and men"

expected and/or personally desired (Lück, Diabaté, and Ruckdeschel 2017, Diabaté and Lück 2014). In this context, role models are a "bundle of socially shared (mental or verbalised) imaginations of a desired or desirable and principally achievable future which are supposed to be realised by corresponding action" (Giesel 2007: 245). This is connected to the concept of cultural life scripts. Such scripts and role models may refer to family issues, such as the "normal" composition of a family or the "perfect" timing of when to have children. A role model can have an impact on individual behavior in three related ways (Lück, Diabaté, and Ruckdeschel 2017, Diabaté and Lück 2014): 1) by the actor's motivation to put their personal desires into practice (like attitudes, preferences or values), 2) by the motivation to fulfil other people's social expectations and to avoid social exclusion (like prescriptive norms referring to social pressure), and 3) by the non-reflective following of routines or social practices in order to save time and effort. However, the leitbild or role model concept assumes that conceptions of normality mostly fulfill all three criteria at the same time and that these are interrelated (Lück, Diabaté, and Ruckdeschel 2017). In this sense, role models are much more complex than most cultural concepts.

A diverse society as the German one certainly does not have a "one and only" Leitbild, but general, reliable tendencies can be identified and addressed. Hence, people have ideas on how the various spheres of everyday life should be. This is also true for family life and its various aspects: partnership, parenthood, childcare, the distribution of work between mothers and fathers.

For Germany as a nation, there are significant differences between individual Leitbilder and Leitbilder perceived in society. According to their individual Leitbild, most Germans between 20 and 39 think it is important that a father should be actively involved in childcare and also reduce his hours of paid work. The perceived cultural Leitbild on a societal level, however, suggests that a responsible father should provide a decent (or at least sufficient) income for the whole family. Furthermore, "stay at home dads" are considered "unnatural" (Lück 2015). Quite obviously, there is a contradiction between individual and cultural Leitbilder. This discordance is explained by the fact that the cultural Leitbild is "intergenerational" and therefore also shaped by older Germans with a more traditional idea of family and fatherhood than the 20 to 39-year-olds who were interviewed for the empirical study (Junck and Lück 2015). Furthermore, the cultural Leitbild is reflected by the institutions (e.g., German tax system favoring traditional families) that (still) adhere to a traditional role model. Hence, there is a coexistence of opposing Leitbilder that can lead to inner conflicts, a lack of orientation and dissatisfaction for the concerned individuals (Lück, Diabaté & Ruckdeschel 2017).

Interestingly, a significant number of men, especially childless men, consider both duties – being active in childcare as a father and providing the family's income – essential (Lück, 2015). This may indicate a lack of orientation that ultimately creates unachievable expectations.

The findings for mothers do not really differ. Most 20 to 39-year-old Germans think that a mother should work for pay (in order to preserve her financial independence), but also spent sufficient time with her children (Lück, Diabaté & Ruckdeschel 2017). Similar to the fathers, but more strongly, mothers experience a conflict between their personal and the cultural Leitbild in society. The traditional idea of family in Germany is strongly linked to the belief that a mother should care for her children personally and not make use of public childcare (Diabaté 2015) (Table 3).

Table 3: Approval of the statement "Children of 1 to 3 years of age suffer when they are predominantly cared for in daycare centers" in East and West Germany, 2012 and 2016

	2012	2016
West Germany	46.3	38.9
East Germany (incl. Berlin)	20.7	15.2

Note: Four-level attitude scale: the categories of "I agree entirely" and "I agree somnewhat" were combined
Source: Familienleitbilder (FLB) 2012 and 2016, weighted

Furthermore, Germans aged 20 to 39 are very concerned about childcare and the responsibilities of "good parents." Hence, 90 percent disagree with the statement that "Children will grow up no matter what, so it's not necessary to put a lot of thought into it" and about 40 percent claim that "Children of 1 to 3 years of age suffer when they are predominantly cared for in day care centers" (Ruckdeschel 2015).

It is not surprising though that some Leitbilder are correlated with people having their own children or not. People who agree with the statement that "Parents can do a lot wrong in raising children, so they should become well informed" show a lesser chance of being a parent by less than 50 percent. This finding can be interpreted in different ways, but a very probable one is that highly demanding imagined parental responsibilities discourage young adults from having children.

With special attention to the situation and persisting or vanishing differences in the Neue Länder and Alte Länder, the Leitbild study offers relevant knowledge concerning mothers and their role in the respective regional society. Although the convergence of fertility patterns is achieved in East and West Germany, it may be premature to stress modernization of the Neue Länder as an explanation as the underlying Leitbilder may differ nonetheless.

With reunification, as mentioned above, the political, economic and administrative sphere underwent an immediate, essential and irreversible change. Society and culture were certainly also affected, but behaviors and attitudes are slower in this regard and may change either quickly or hardly at all depending on each individual. Furthermore, people's attitudes are shaped by biographical and societal experience and embeddedness. Attitudes that were promoted and internalized in the GDR's society not only proved stable but were also passed on to ensuing generations (Nauck et. al. 1995). Hence, the question to what extent GDR-shaped attitudes and patterns of behavior remain persistent is relevant in order to better understand German reunification in demographic terms, as well. Bernardi (2007) and Boehnke (2013) argue that this effect of intergenerational transfer is significant while Huinink (2012) generally agrees to this view but points out that two dimensions need to be addressed: the intergenerational/inter-cohort perspective, which leads to a preservation of "old" habits, and the necessity of unavoidable changes in behavior due to the new conditions in reunified Germany. Both spheres are interdependent.

After reunification, the East German population in the Neue Länder did not simply adapt West German values, attitudes and norms, but maintained older, GDR-like patterns and developed new specific attitudes that are visibly influenced by the GDR experience (Schiefer & Naderi 2015). A typically East German, GDR-shaped attitude towards partnership and family is the desire to have children/become a parent (especially for women)

(Boehnke 2013). Furthermore, (full or part time) work and family life for women/mother-hood are neither a contradiction nor burden or disgrace for women in the Neue Länder. Both work (career) and children are a central aspect of East German women's individual life script and self-concept. This attitude is linked to the GDR society and socialist ideology, where women were considered an integral part of the workforce. Being employed full time was also an (ideological) marker of equal rights. Thus, motherhood and work for women were actively supported by the GDR government, which also put emphasis on the creation of infrastructure for this specific kind of life (Schiefer & Naderi 2015). Some authors argue that the high value of the core family (parents and children) is also due to the repressive system of the GDR; family life provided (psychological) shelter, relief and relaxation from the demanding everyday routine in socialist society (Stöbel-Richter 2010). This high esteem of family and children continued as a Leitbild after reunification and childlessness is lower in the Neue Länder (Goldstein & Kreyenfeld 2011).

In the Alte Länder, however, such a modern role model – from today's point of view of globalization – had not evolved. Mothers were (and are) subject to extensive normative expec-tations with regard to childcare and motherhood. Motherhood is perceived as a "full-time job," not leaving any leeway for paid work. Bringing up children and parenting should be left to the parents (namely the mother) and – if possible – not be "outsourced" to nannies or a kindergarten. Kindergarten as a part time activity is perceived acceptable from three years of age at the earliest. Women with full-time jobs and children in day nursery were even subject to social stigma and called "bad mothers" (Ruckdeschel 2009). Hence, the West German model implies a decision between motherhood or career. Furthermore, the father is deemed responsible for taking care of all financial needs, thus paid full time work. This attitude is changing, but still remains a visible Leitbild in the Alte Länder nevertheless. Therefore, the division of labor among couples in Germany exhibits a distinct (and persistent) east-west divide (Table 4) with a much higher rate of full-time working mothers in the Neue Länder.

Table 4: Division of labor among couples in Germany 2015 (%)

	Parents with youngest child between 3 and 6 years of age		All couples up to 65 years of age
	Alte Länder	Neue Länder	Germany
Sole earner, male	21	12	16
Supplementary earner, female	47	16	27
Both in full time jobs	18	57	36
Both in part time jobs	2	2	2
Other variants	11	12	19

Source: Statistisches Bundesamt 2017, Mikrozensus

Thus, Neue and Alte Länder exhibit relatively differing attitudes especially with regard to the role of mothers. Leitbild research has proven that about 20 years after reunification, these differences can still be ascertained. Empirical Leitbild research from 2012 and 2016 shows that the desire among young people to have children is similar in both parts of Germany. However, it is in the Neue Länder that this desire is realized, while childlessness (although the idea of having children and starting a family is very important for young women) proves significantly more frequent in the Alte Länder. As Schiefer & Naderi (2015) showed, compared to West German women in the ages between 30 and 39 years, women in the Neue Länder tend to have less unfulfilled desires for children (are more likely to be mothers...).

When asked whether having their own children is very important to them, 100 percent of East German mothers and 87 percent of childless women agreed (Schiefer & Naderi 2015). In West Germany, this proportion is lower with 98 percent of mothers and 79 percent of childless women agreeing to this statement. What is especially striking is the rather large difference of opinion among childless persons in the Neue and Alte Länder. Childlessness in general appears to be more socially accepted in West Germany. This difference can be related to the East German "matter-of-factness" of having children, as the idea of being a mother is highly valued and other external societal norms about motherhood or whether mothers should work are largely overweighed by the "value" of children and the family. In West Germany, however, normative aspects such as the rather strict notion of a caring "full-time" mother and the decision between a career or motherhood lead to a postponement of births or even childlessness despite a positive attitude towards family and motherhood.

Therefore, research has shown that women in the Neue Länder have a more family- and motherhood-oriented attitude but reject the traditional idea of being a financially dependent "stay-at-home-mother." However, in the Alte and Neue Länder, respondents fully agree to the idea that raising children is a demanding task that requires great devotion by the parents. The difference concerns the Leitbild of which form of partnership such an environment is given and whether women should/could work and have their children in childcare facilities during the workdays or not. This also means that inherited ideas on more or less traditional role models prevail in each part of Germany and convergence is not yet in sight. On the contrary: the more modern model of the Neue Länder appears much better suited to post-modernity in a global-ized world than the "old fashioned" West German perception, which is losing importance.

2.2   Mortality and life expectancy (Michael Mühlichen, BiB)

West and East Germany experienced significant differences in the development of mortality over recent decades. In the first years after the division of Germany, average life expec-tancy was on the same level in the FRG and the GDR. According to the earliest available numbers of the German Federal Statistical Office (Statistisches Bundesamt 2012), average life expectancy at birth for men was 65.06 years in the GDR in 1952/1953 and 64.56 in the FRG in 1949/1951. Among women, it was 69.07 in the GDR and 68.48 in the FRG in those years.[3] Between the late 1970s and 1990, however, a remarkable gap to the disadvantage of the GDR had emerged. After reunification, this east-west gradient in mortality began to vanish, but it is still evident to a lesser degree among men.

Thus, convergence is the dominating trend when the development of mortality in the Neue Länder compared to the Alte Länder is studied. This is mainly linked to a decrease in avoidable mortality since the de facto quality of the healthcare system in the Neue Länder has increased and has finally reached an equal standard with the Alte Länder (Nolte et al. 2002; Kibele and Scholz 2009).

---

[3]   Values for East and West Germany with the same time reference and underlying methods are only available for the period as of 1956 through the Human Mortality Database (HMD).

Because of the obvious impact of political separation and reunification on German mortality development, especially regarding the long-term consequences of different healthcare systems, the German example has been considered a "natural experiment" in demographic research (Vaupel et al. 2003; Vogt and Vaupel 2015). Based on a Lee-Carter model, Vogt (2013) measured that the fall of the Berlin Wall – with its accompanying medical, economic and socio-structural consequences – added 4 years to female and 5.7 years to male life expectancy at birth in East Germany between 1990 and 2009.

In the following, this chapter describes this differing mortality development in East and West Germany and its drivers with a special focus on life expectancy, regional differences and causes of death.

2.2.1   Life expectancy at birth and remaining life expectancy at age 65

The east-west gradient in life expectancy began to develop in the late 1970s and grew to 3.4 years among men and 2.7 years among women in 1990. Since reunification, this gap has decreased considerably. Full convergence has been reached among the female population in recent years, whereas the male population in East Germany still exhibits a lower life expectancy (1.2 years). The process of adaptation in life expectancy took place in the 1990s especially, whereas further equalization has been comparatively small since 2000 (Figure 17).

Figure 17: Average life expectancy at birth in East and West Germany by sex 1956–2015

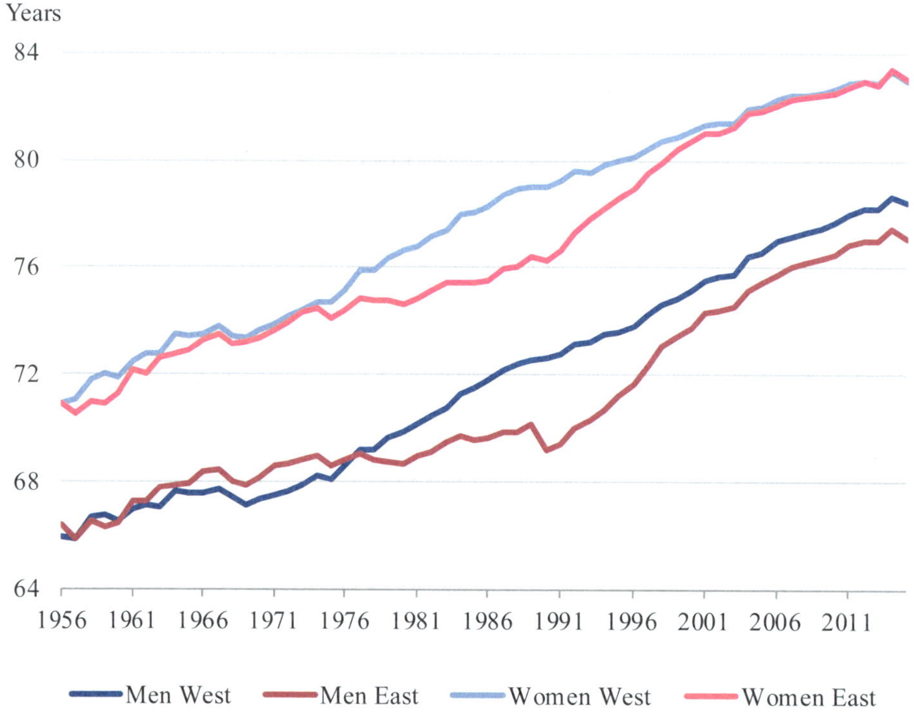

Source: Human Mortality Database (as of March 29, 2017)

The main driver for the divergence in the 1970s and 1980s as well as for the convergence after reunification was the state of health care. Because the GDR hardly profited from "Western" innovations in medical technology as of the 1970s in the treatment of cardiovascular diseases, the increase of life expectancy in the GDR was comparatively poor. After reunification, however, rapid modernization of the medical infrastructure boosted the increase of life expectancy in the former GDR, which also becomes visible in a considerable decrease of amenable and old-age mortality, especially in connection with cardiovascular diseases (Dinkel 2003; Gjonça et al. 2000; Nolte et al. 2002; Kibele and Scholz 2009). The remaining gradient in life expectancy among men is strongly connected to socio-economic conditions like higher unemployment in East Germany (Scholz et al. 2010; Kibele 2012). Lifestyle factors such as smoking and alcohol abuse are further important causes for this gap among men (Kibele and Scholz 2009; Kibele 2012; Luy 2004; Mons 2011), whereas higher smoking rates among West German women compared to East German women have supported the rapid convergence among women in spite of worse living conditions (Myrskylä and Scholz 2013). This "advantage" of East German women will, however, presumably change to the opposite when the younger cohorts of East German women, who show dramatically higher smoking rates than previous ones, reach the mortality-relevant age (Vogt et al. 2017). Other important context factors are the lower accessibility of medical care in peripheral regions of East Germany and selective emigration of "good risks" from East to West Germany (Behrendt 2010; Kibele 2012; Luy and Caselli 2007).

The development of further life expectancy at age 65 is very similar to that at age 0 (Figure 18). The gradient between East and West Germany is greatly linked with higher levels of cardiovascular mortality in East Germany. Cardiovascular diseases are the dominating causes of death at older ages and are fostered by poorer socio-economic conditions in the east and poorer accessibility of adequate and timely medical care in the peripheral regions of East Germany (Kibele and Scholz 2009; Behrendt 2010; Kibele 2012). Another reason is the poorer general life conditions during the GDR era, which East German people at age 65 and older experienced for a long period of their lives (Dinkel 2003). But the rapid increase in life expectancy after reunification even at ages 80 and older shows the importance of late-life events as well (Gjonça et al. 2000).

Figure 18: Average remaining life expectancy at age 65 in East and West Germany by sex 1956–2015

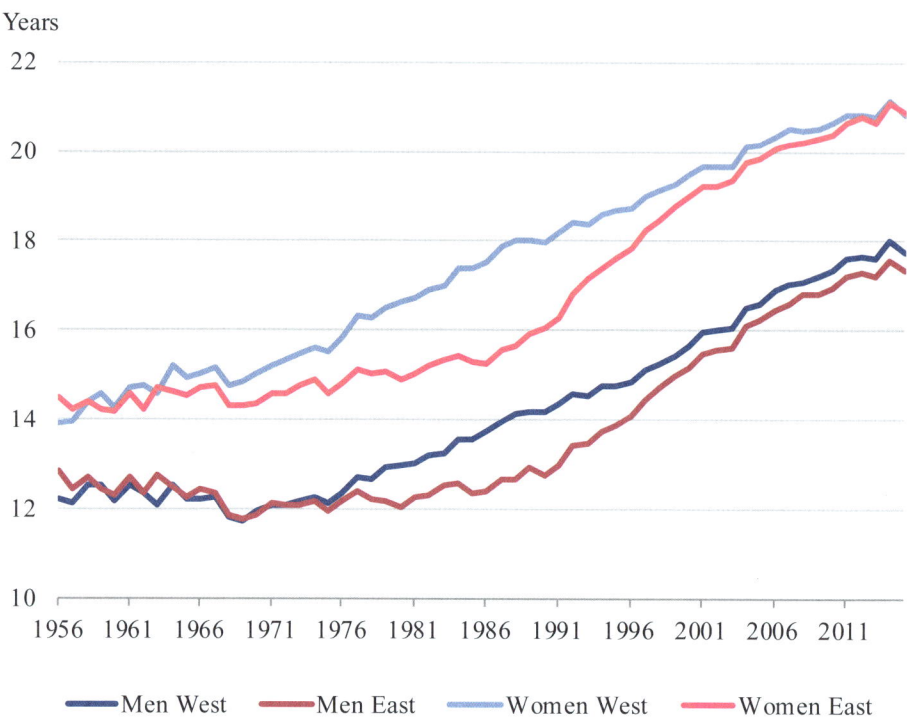

Source: Human Mortality Database (as of March 29, 2017)

2.2.2 Regional mortality differences

Whereas the east-west gradient in mortality declined considerably after reunification, another gradient has become more prominent: the gap between northern and southern Germany, which becomes visible on the regional level. In both the Alte Länder and Neue Länder, average life expectancy is higher in the south (Table 5). For instance, Sachsen exhibits a higher average life expectancy than Mecklenburg-Vorpommern and Baden-Württemberg exhibits a higher life expectancy than Schleswig-Holstein. On the one hand, this is due to higher mortality from neoplasms in northern Germany, which is much related to the higher tobacco consumption of northern German men and women (Mons 2011). On the other hand, socio-economic conditions are better in the southern part of the country, which particularly adds to the lower mortality level of southern German men (Latzitis 2011; Kibele 2012). Another explanatory factor that is more related to East Germany is the accessibility of timely and adequate health care, which is better in the more urbanized south (Bucher 2002; Mai 2004). Thus, mortality from heart attack or stroke is still comparatively high in the peripheral regions of East Germany (Kibele 2012).

Table 5: Average life expectancy at birth in the German Länder

a) Men

	1982/84		1990/92		2000/02		2013/15
Baden-Württemberg	72.02	↗	73.88	↗	76.79	↗	79.52
Bayern	71.07	↗	73.18	↗	75.96	↗	78.93
Bremen	70.28	↗	72.29	↗	74.67	↗	76.82
Hamburg	70.45	↗	72.35	↗	75.68	↗	78.29
Hessen	71.52	↗	73.44	↗	76.20	↗	78.76
Niedersachsen	71.10	↗	73.02	↗	75.39	↗	77.84
Nordrhein-Westfalen	70.40	↗	72.57	↗	75.34	↗	77.88
Rheinland-Pfalz	70.59	↗	72.80	↗	75.59	↗	78.35
Saarland	69.55	↗	71.70	↗	74.44	↗	77.15
Schleswig-Holstein	71.30	↗	73.11	↗	75.60	↗	78.00
Berlin	68.62	↗	70.94	↗	75.24	↗	77.76
Brandenburg	68.92	↘	68.85	↗	74.08	↗	77.38
Mecklenburg-Vorpommern	68.33	↘	67.84	↗	73.14	↗	76.54
Sachsen	-		70.42	↗	74.85	↗	77.58
Sachsen-Anhalt	-		68.94	↗	73.34	↗	76.17
Thüringen	69.58	↗	70.05	↗	74.43	↗	77.17
Germany	-		72.09	↗	75.38	↗	78.18

↓

Table 5: Average life expectancy at birth in the German Länder – continued

b) Women

	1982/84		1990/92		2000/02		2013/15
Baden-Württemberg	78.41	↗	80.10	↗	82.27	↗	83.90
Bayern	77.60	↗	79.45	↗	81.64	↗	83.52
Bremen	77.66	↗	79.03	↗	80.80	↗	82.34
Hamburg	77.25	↗	79.26	↗	81.38	↗	83.00
Hessen	77.84	↗	79.65	↗	81.57	↗	83.21
Niedersachsen	77.80	↗	79.54	↗	81.24	↗	82.77
Nordrhein-Westfalen	77.20	↗	79.15	↗	80.97	↗	82.52
Rheinland-Pfalz	77.16	↗	79.15	↗	81.25	↗	82.93
Saarland	76.47	↗	78.44	↗	80.35	↗	82.13
Schleswig-Holstein	77.63	↗	79.24	↗	81.23	↗	82.79
Berlin	75.28	↗	77.35	↗	81.09	↗	83.02
Brandenburg	75.18	↗	76.56	↗	80.83	↗	82.94
Mecklenburg-Vorpommern	75.12	↗	76.05	↗	80.52	↗	82.88
Sachsen	-		77.21	↗	81.50	↗	83.58
Sachsen-Anhalt	-		76.34	↗	80.31	↗	82.45
Thüringen	75.18	↗	76.85	↗	80.73	↗	83.02
Germany	-		78.68	↗	81.22	↗	83.06

Source: Kibele (2012: 65) for German Länder 1982/84–2000/02; Statistisches Bundesamt (2016) for Germany and German Länder 2013/15; Statistisches Bundesamt (2012) for Germany 2000/02; Human Mortality Database (state of 29 March 2017) for Germany 1991

2.2.3 Main causes of death

All cause of death groups have decreased in recent decades in both West and East Germany but to a different degree and with the exception of the group of mental, behavioral and neuro-developmental disorders, which has increased in all German Länder. Due to different coding practices, the development of causes of death prior to reunification is not fully comparable between East and West Germany (Luy 2004). The slight increase in death rates in 2011 is largely due to corrected population numbers as a consequence of the 2011 census.

Both West and East Germany have experienced a decrease in old-age mortality in recent decades. This decrease is largely connected to a decrease in mortality from cardiovascular diseases (Figure 19). These diseases have been the leading cause of death group in Germany in recent decades and particularly affect retirement age. Comparing Alte Länder and Neue Länder, there is a trend of convergence. However, full convergence has not yet been reached. The higher cardiovascular mortality in East Germany is linked to its more rural settlement structure. There are higher levels in peripheral areas since timely access to medical care has room for improvement there and is especially important in cases of heart attacks and strokes, for instance (Bucher 2002; Mai 2004). Among men, socio-economic differences – particularly the more unfavorable labor market situation in the east – play an important part as well (Scholz et al. 2010; Kibele 2012).

Figure 19: Mortality from cardiovascular diseases in East and West Germany by sex, standardized death rate 1980–2015

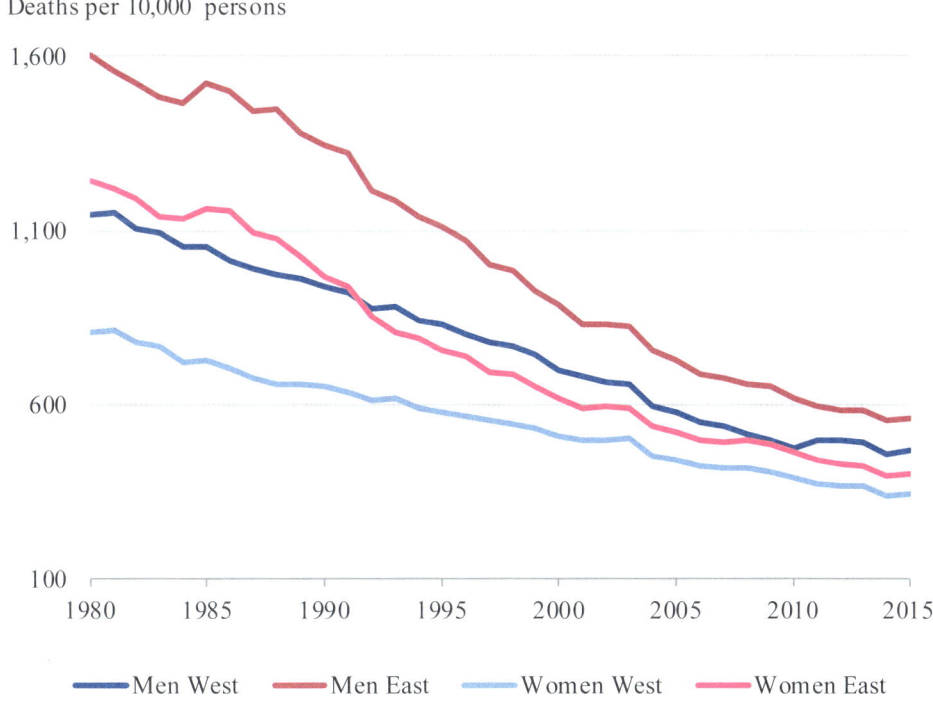

Deaths per 10,000 persons

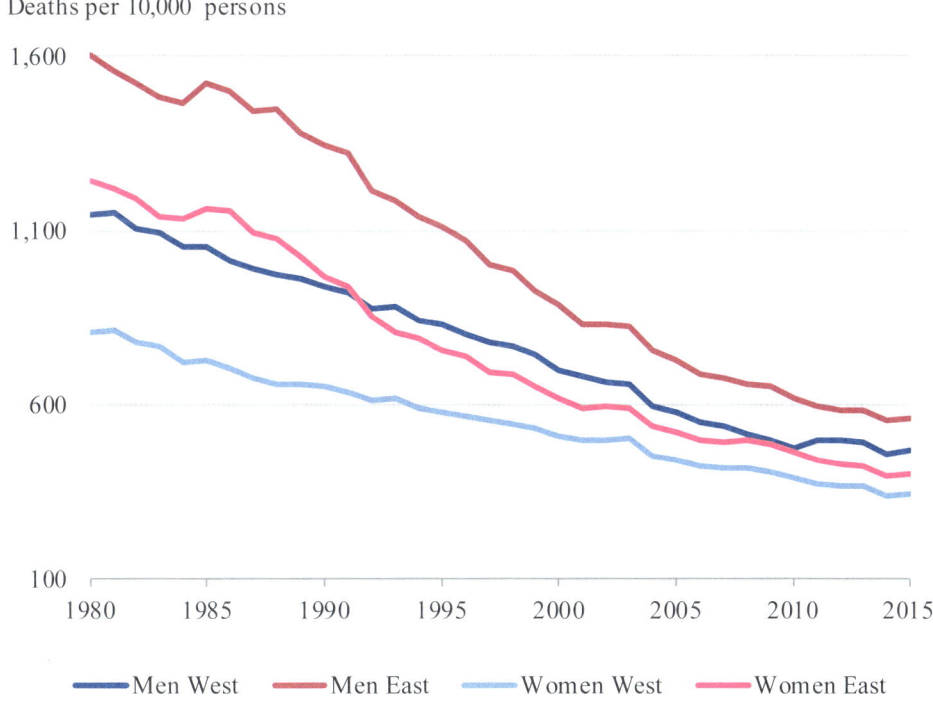

Note: Both East and West Germany without Berlin as of 1998 due to data restrictions; European Standard Population 2013

Source: Statistisches Bundesamt 2017, Gesundheitsberichterstattung des Bundes

The different coding practices of the GDR compared to the FRG become especially obvious in the study of neoplasms, which are the second-most common cause of death group in Germany (Figure 20). After applying the western coding practice, the level of mortality from neoplasms shifted in East Germany to the level of West Germany. Ever since, mortality from neoplasms decreased in East and West Germany but not to the same degree as cardiovascular diseases. Differences between east and west are comparatively low and are strongly related to smoking behavior. Smoking rates are higher among East German men than West German men and higher among West German women than East German women, at least with regard to the middle adult ages that are relevant for cancer deaths (Mons 2011; Robert-Koch-Institut 2011; Myrskylä and Scholz 2013).

Figure 20: Mortality from neoplasms in East and West Germany by sex, standardized death rate 1980–2015

Deaths per 10,000 persons

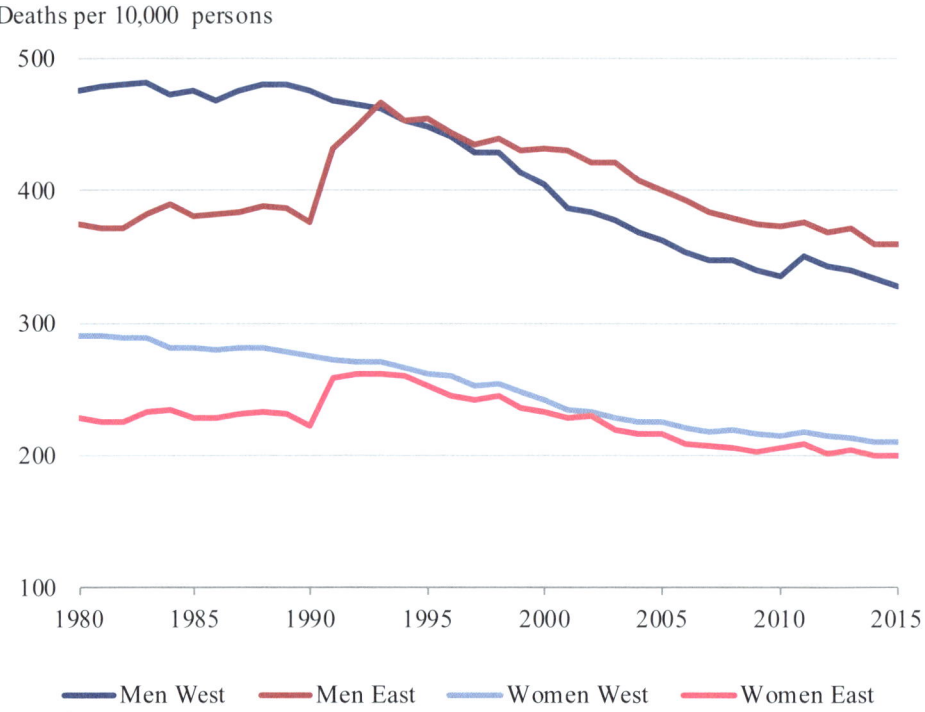

Note: Both East and West Germany without Berlin as of 1998 due to data restrictions; European Standard Population 2013

Source: Statistisches Bundesamt 2017, Gesundheitsberichterstattung des Bundes

Other important cause of death groups are respiratory diseases, mental disorders, digestive diseases and external causes. But the numbers for these causes are relatively low compared to cardiovascular diseases and neoplasms. Among external causes, however, the development of traffic accidents and suicides is particularly interesting as it shows almost full convergence between east and west although the gap was comparatively large at the time of reunification. The drastic rise in fatal traffic accidents in East Germany directly after the fall of the Berlin Wall, most prominently among men, is a consequence of the interaction of the sudden availability of faster cars and the unfavorable condition of East German streets, especially in the north of East Germany with its many narrow tree-lined roads that were not compatible with higher speeds. Therefore, traffic accidents in East Germany ended fatally comparatively often in the early 1990s. But, due to massive improvements of the road network, mortality from traffic accidents dramatically declined in East Germany, although it is still comparatively higher in its northern part (Gärtner and Mühlichen 2012).

One cause of death that significantly differed in East and West Germany before reunification is suicide. Although the suicide rates were decreasing in both states in the 1980s, East Germany showed a considerably higher level. After reunification, the levels between the two regions have equalized among women. Among men, however, suicide mortality is still higher in the eastern part, but to a much lesser degree. It is very likely that the higher levels in the GDR before the fall of the Berlin Wall were partly due to political motives of people who saw no satisfying future for themselves in a locked communist country. However, this correlation has not yet been clearly proven. Some government functionaries and other officials killed themselves after the fall of the Berlin Wall and the collapse of the GDR, which probably contributed to the slight increase in 1991. Fear of investigations against them, the feeling of not being needed anymore or the fact that the political system they believed in had no future were possible motives. But, as mentioned above, there is no massive increase of suicides connected to the system change that would affect the statistics. Contrary to that, the trend in decreasing suicides continued and even accelerated in the early 1990s.

2.3   Migration in divided and reunified Germany

Like the current situation in the DPRK, one of the most (in-) famous specifics of the GDR was total control of and severe restrictions to international migration of their citizens. Citizens of the GDR were not allowed to leave the country whenever they liked. "Republikflucht" (fleeing the republic) was illegal and the border to the Federal Republic of Germany was hermetically closed and successively secured with mines and automatic shooting devices. Illegal crossers of the border were at high risk of being shot. While emigration was practically illegal, international immigration also played only a minor role for the GDR. This was mainly due to the lack of appeal of this authoritarian socialist state with a reputation for a modest standard of living compared to western countries. The situation in this respect changed for a short period in the late 1980s, when workers, mainly from Vietnam, Poland and Mozambique, were temporarily recruited because of a lack of workforce. The total number of international immigrants was less than 200,000 in 1989 (Bade & Oltmer 2004). Even after reunification, the Neue Länder were an exception to the immigration-shaped demographics of Germany, which will be explained below. Internal migration – including the special phenomenon of GDR-FRG migration – is of special relevance for Germany, however.

2.3.1   Patterns of GDR internal migration and the special case of the GDR-FRG migration regime

Before 1990, internal migration mainly moved to the economic and urban agglomerations in the west and south of the FRG (Statistische Ämter des Bundes und der Länder (2015). Furthermore, massive suburbanization had shaped the West German agglomerations since the late 1960s until approximately 2000, when re-urbanization became a trend all over Germany. The GDR, however, exhibits a slightly different pattern, where migration was indirectly determined by government decisions on the development, location and relocation of economic facilities and housing development. Along general lines, internal migration in the GDR was oriented towards the capital city of Berlin, the economic core zones of today's Sachsen and Thüringen and selected newly established and developed economic (often mono-structural) hubs in more rural and peripheral regions (Freitag et. al 1989). This was due to intentions for regional development and partially for tactical reasons (new towns such as Schwedt/Oder and Eisenhüttenstadt were deliberately located far away from the inner-German border). A phenomenon such as suburbanization did not exist, as the housing market was state-controlled. On the other hand, migration on micro level (within cities/ towns) could be temporarily important, when new, big housing projects were completed.

GDR-FRG internal (or quasi-internal) migration from 1950 until 1990 is a special case. Despite antithetic forms of society and a hostile attitude towards the respective other in political terms, migratory flows between the two German states did always exist.

Immediately after the GDR was founded as a socialist state controlled by the Soviet Union, people started leaving the country in high numbers towards the FRG. A peak is marked by the year 1953 (which was also the year of a major uprising against the regime that was eventually put down), when about 331,000 GDR refugees arrived in West Germany (Martens 2010). People in the GDR were dissatisfied with the political system, forcible collectivization of private land and assets in agriculture. Furthermore, they witnessed the better economic development in the FRG. Thus the migratory balance between both Germanys was positive for the FRG with an inflow of rather young and well-educated East Germans. West-east migration, however, (e.g., by West German communists) was always a niche phenomenon.

Between 1949 and 1961, about 2.7 million people left the GDR (Martens 2010). Given a total population of about 17 million in 1960 and the effect of brain drain, the dimension of flight became threatening to the regime. As a consequence, state borders were hermetically closed in August 1961 and not reopened until November 1989 to prevent further emigration. GDR citizens were only allowed to leave the country with explicit approval by the state administration. Hence, from 1962 until 1988, the total number of persons emigrating from the GDR only amounts to 625,000 (Martens 2010), most of them leaving their homeland legally, after a long and difficult expatriation procedure.

In 1988, when the regime started to erode, massive emigration was an important epiphenomenon related to the failure of the state. An estimated 880,000 people chose to undertake gradual migration via Hungary, the CSSR and sometimes Poland to the FRG in the years 1988 and 1989 before the opening of the border (Wehler 2008). In total between 4.5 and 5 million people emigrated from 1949 until 1989 to the FRG, which represents a quarter of GDR's population in 1950, when the state was founded.

With the fall of the Iron Curtain, emigration to West Germany immediately took place. Exact data on east-west migration from November of 1989 until reunification less than 11 months later are not available. The GDR administration was unable to keep track of the migration flows. Emigration to the FRG was so massive – between 2,000 and 3,000 persons per day (Schröder 2014) – that the Federal government of West Germany was already discussing and planning an economic and monetary union of both German states in December of 1989 in order to diminish one major reason for the migration flows. It is important to note that the main intention of the early monetary union with rather favorable conditions for the GDR was to prevent more and more people from resettling (and indirectly destabilizing both countries). This purely politically motivated "Wirtschafts-, Währungs- und Sozialunion (WWSU)" entered into force on July 1, 1990 and made the Deutsche Mark (DM; West German currency) the common and only currency in the (still existing) GDR. It also created the basis for implementing the FRG-type social market economy and paved the way to rapid reunification. A certain amount of GDR money was exchanged 1:1 per person (the thresholds were 6,000 DM for people over 60 years of age, 4,000 DM for adults and 2,000 DM per child under 14 years of age). Savings above these limits were exchanged at a rate of 2 GDR Mark to 1 DM. The same rate was applied to debts. Salaries, retirement pensions, rental rates and other recurring financial liabilities were rated 1:1. Although the effective exchange rate of FRG to GDR money based on the underlying economic benchmarks is difficult to estimate, it is clear that it was less than it was agreed upon in the monetary union.

When this monetary union was officially announced in early 1990, migration started to decline and only about 2,000 people per week (Schröder 2014) left the GDR to the FRG until reunification on October 1, 1990, which shows it was a successful measure. The monetary union, which was backed by massive subsidies and monetary flows, including shares from an additional 5 percent income tax "of solidarity" (Solidaritätszuschlag) on the annual taxation, must be seen as an important basis for successful reunification and social harmony.

2.3.2   Internal migration since reunification

Migration from the Neue Länder to the Alte Länder remained a long-term and urging phenomenon even after the immediate reunification era. For at least one decade after German reunification, living conditions and economic prospects in east and west were too different despite very rapid alignment of the general conditions since 1990. Between 1990 and 2015 more than 4 million people moved from the Neue to the Alte Länder. 25 years after reunification, the balance is clearly negative from an East German perspective. Migration from the Alte Länder to the Neue Länder certainly is also significant, especially since the turn of the millennium but – in retrospect – is still outnumbered by the east-west movers.

However, the massive losses, which occurred especially in the first few years after reunification, did not remain at a continuous high level but exhibited more or less accentuated variations with peaks in the early 1990s and just after 2000. Exactly 15 years after reunification, migration between the Alte and Neue Länder is more or less balanced. This is a very recent trend and its long-term stability is not yet clear (Figure 21).

Neoclassic economic theory would presuppose a correlation between regional disparities on the labor market and the direction and total volume of migration. Actually, Germany is known to be an example where regional disparities in local development and the labor market as well as unemployment generally do explain the patterns of internal migration (Kupizewski & Rees 1998). Then again, we know that simple push-pull theories can help to understand migration flows on a macro level but, as mentioned, just in a general, if not to say superficial, way. Decisions concerning migration are complex processes on an individual level including compromises and hazards. Thus, migration theories are far from being fully comprehensive. Furthermore, this prototypical link between job market and migration in Germany is especially shaped by the disparities between the Alte and Neue Länder (Schlömer & Bucher 2001).

Figure 21: Migration in thousands between East and West Germany 1991–2015

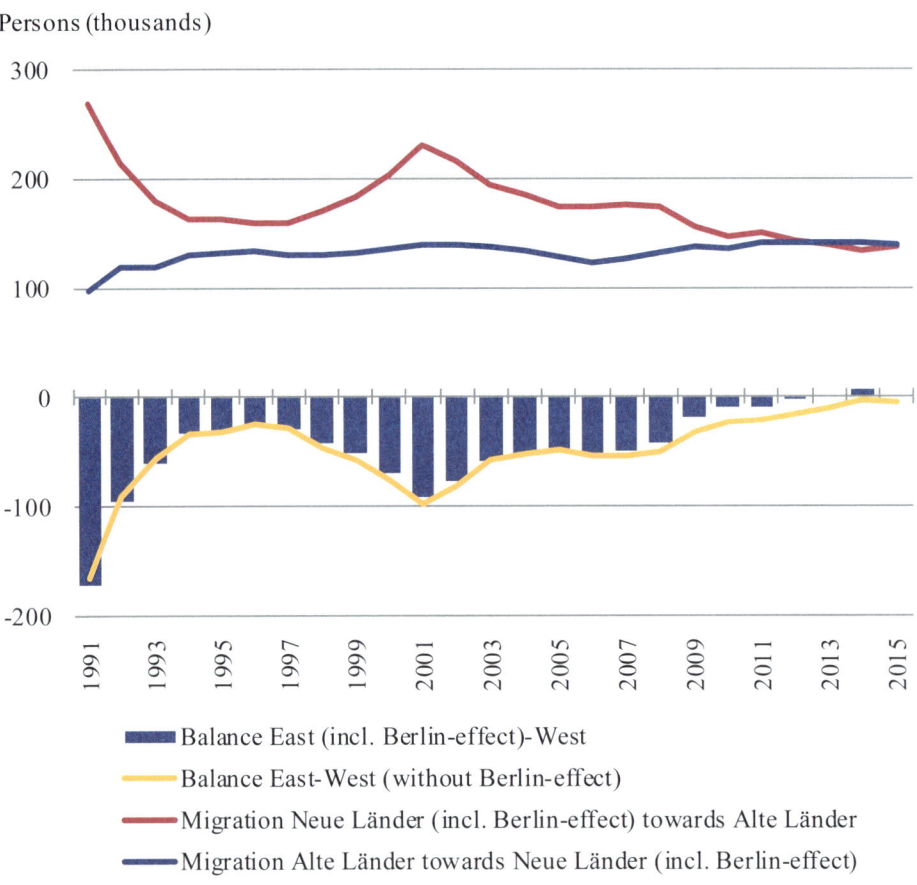

Source: Statistisches Bundesamt 2017

With regard to migration between the Neue Länder and Alte Länder and the capital city of Berlin, it is obvious that uneven economic development, unemployment, standards of living and job opportunities account for most of the outbound migration from the Neue Länder to the Alte Länder (Figure 22).

Furthermore, weekly (mostly long distance) commuting became a lasting and common phenomenon in the Neue Länder (Table 6).

Figure 22: Internal migration balance (%) of German Länder 1991-2015

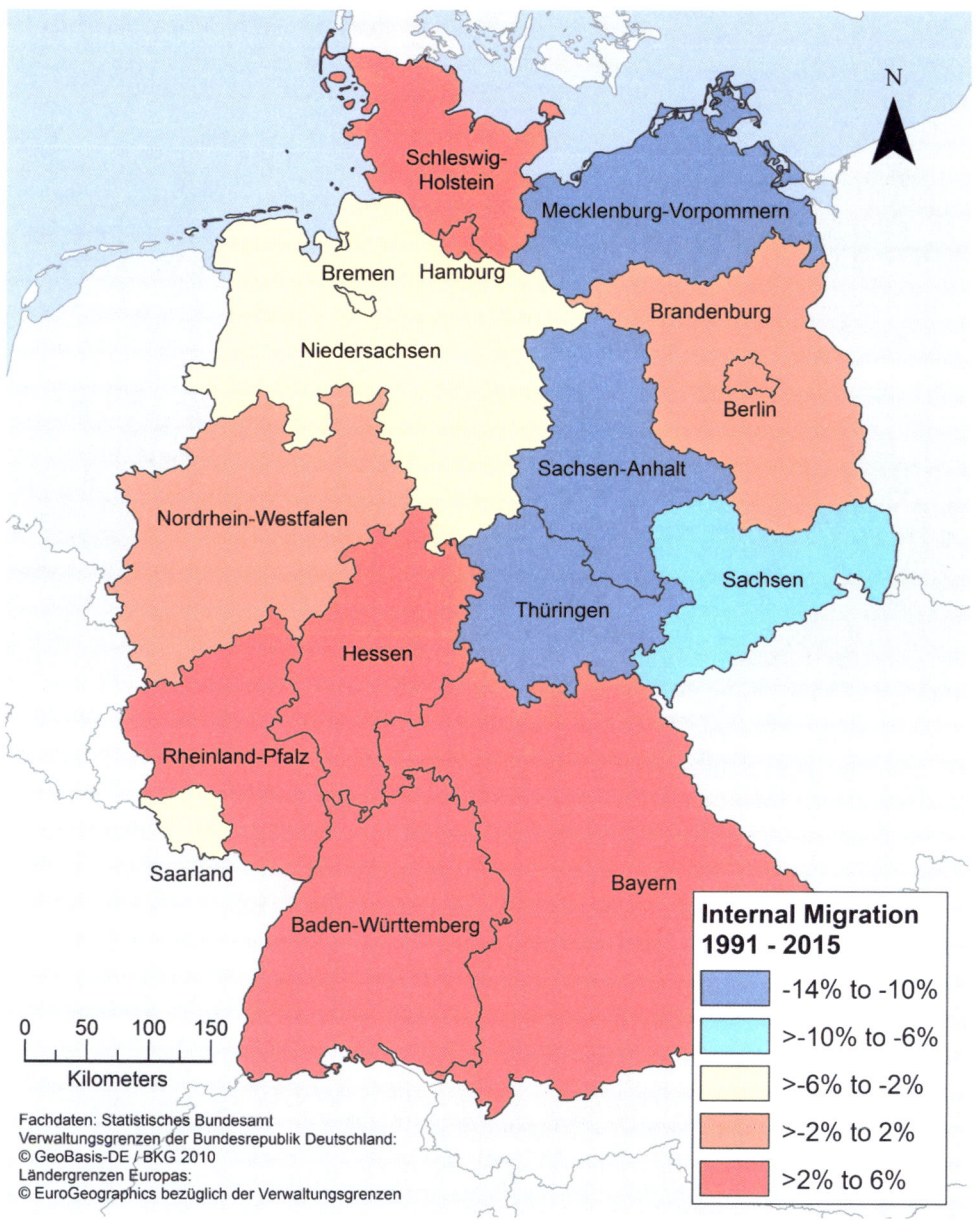

Table 6: Job-related commuting between the Neue Länder and Alte Länder 2000-2016

	2000	2005	2010	2016
Job related commuters (employees) Alte Länder ⇨ Neue Länder	137,800	137,700	186,100	278,000
Share of those commuters among all employees in Germany	0.50	0.53	0.68	0.90
Job related commuters (employees) Neue Länder ⇨ Alte Länder	599,700	618,800	643,700	662,600
Share of those commuters among all employees in Germany	2.17	2.37	2.35	2.14

Source: Statistisches Bundesamt 2017

Given the fact that East German residents account for 6,023,000 persons out of 30,951,000 German employees in total, an impressive proportion of 2 percent commutes to the Alte Länder for work.

Nonetheless, unemployment itself is not typically related to migration in East Germany. Unemployed people tend to be even less mobile, although emigration could change their individual unfavorable situations (Grundmann 1994). Furthermore, a cluster analysis by Schlömer and Bucher (2001) revealed that the economically weakest regions with highest unemployment rates in East Germany did not have the highest migration rates. High unemployment rates, weak job markets in the Neue Länder and migration to the Alte Länder are generally related, but the respective correlation proved moderate. This is due to the fact that push-pull models are too uneven and the neoclassical understanding of economy and migration is a little too bold. Also, migrants are far from being fully informed optimizers (with theoretically highest migration rates out of the most peripheral regions towards the strongest regions with the most promising job market, as a result) but often try to minimize effort in the sense of being satisfiers. Hence, as a consequence, Schlömer and Bucher (2001) show that in the first decade after reunification, east-west migrants were more likely to settle in one of the Alte Länder that was relatively close to their former home region, regardless of the job market situation and risk of unemployment. Also, regions within the Neue Länder with more promising perspectives than at home but far from being as (objectively) promising as the strongest regions in the Alte Länder represented important destinations for a move.

Furthermore, people leaving the Neue Länder were mainly those who were already well established and found even better conditions and opportunities aligned to their qualifications in the Alte Länder. Moreover, impending unemployment tends to be another reason to leave.

Two major waves of east-west migration can be distinguished. The first one took place immediately after the fall of the Berlin Wall and the second one peaked in 2001 and coincided with "economic stagnation in the East and improving job prospects in the West" (Heiland 2004: 188). This out-migration was highest among young (Figure 23), well-qualified adults (Peukert and Smolny 2011).

Figure 23: Migration balance Neue Länder with Alte Länder 1991-2015, absolute cases,
           age groups

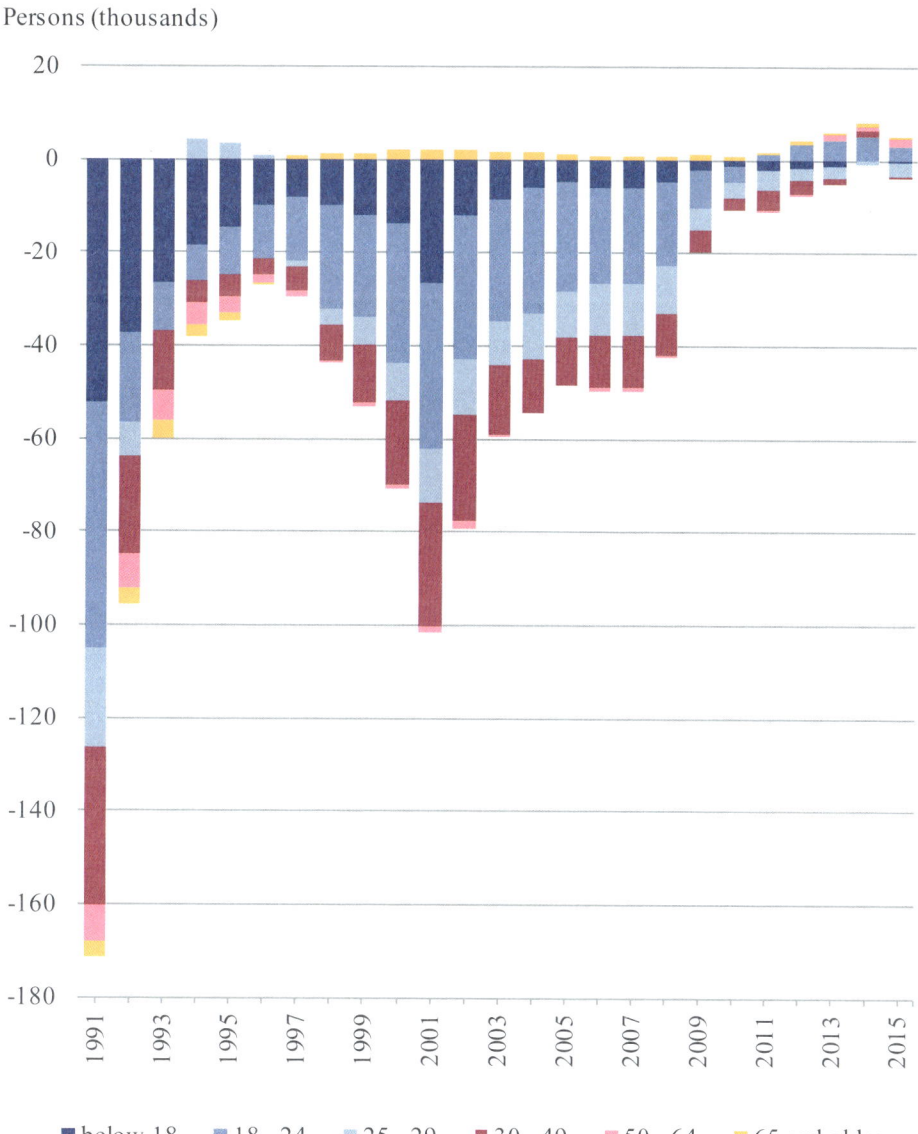

Persons (thousands)

Source: Statistisches Bundesamt 2017

Although massive east-west movement is as major characteristic linked to reunification, this dominance must not obstruct our view on the opposite direction: migration from the Alte Länder to the Neue Länder since 1990. Much lower in intensity, this flux is accentuated and developed distinct patterns as it mainly moved to the urban stability poles of the Neue Länder. In the beginning, mainly government clerks, administrative personnel and entrepreneurs from the Alte Länder were moving to the Neue Länder, thus it was a phenomenon of highly qualified persons in managerial positions. Gradually students, retirees and "re-settlers" became a distinct group of west-east migrants. An empirical study done by Jain and Schmithals (2009) using the example of the city of Magdeburg, Sachsen-Anhalt, showed the main motivations for those coming to the Neue Länder. About half of the immigrants were returning East Germans and the other half immigrants from West Germany. Most of the latter were rather young and more than two-thirds were students. The returnees were mainly retired persons coming back "home." Most returnees mentioned personal links and only one-third moved because of job opportunities. The younger people, however, did not intend to stay for a longer period of time.

Both the number of east-west migrants and the number of west-east migrants have been higher among men than among women since reunification. Although more men emigrated from east to west than women, the proportion of women in East Germany decreased among the working-age population in the 1990s and 2000s. This is because considerably fewer women than men moved from west to east in this period.

In the time span since reunification, almost 4.5 million people moved from the Neue Länder to the Alte Länder, but 3.3 million people also migrated from west to the east.

"Brain drain" of young, educated people in particular became a major challenge in peripheral regions of the Neue Länder, with skilled young females being even more likely to leave (Kühntopf & Stedtfeld 2012; Maretzke 2009). Weiß (2006) points out that brain drain represents an imminent threat in peripheral regions, significantly and lastingly disturbing social cohesion in the affected places. Friedrich (2008) acknowledges the threat of brain drain and societal disruption through out-migration-related demographic change, but predicted the current slow-down rather early, based on the gradually declining losses in the Neue Länder's migration balance since 2000 and inner-East German tendencies of re-urbanization and demographic stabilization of the urban agglomerations, which will be explained more in detail below.

Within the Neue Länder, internal migration in the first decade after reunification was shaped by massive suburbanization, which shattered the city centers demographically, socially and economically (Dangschat et. al. 2001). The term "shrinking city" became a synonym for "East German city." Around the turn of the millennium, this trend declined to a rather low level. That said, the major cities in the Neue Länder are currently displaying patterns of re-urbanization. This re-urbanization is a visible trend since about 2005 and the major cities in the Neue Länder started to become poles of economic and demographic growth within a continuously shrinking hinterland. This trend reversal for East German urban poles with striking growth rates after more than a decade of demographic decline is positive, but we should not forget that the (statistical) base from which regrowth started was rather low. None of East German major cities – with the exception of Berlin – has yet caught up with its demographic structure and weight before 1990.

Current data seems to confirm the hypothesis of a "new era" in east-west migration without a striking disequilibrium. A closer look, however, reveals that the positive balance for the Neue Länder since 2013 is almost exclusively linked to migration into East German cities, partially including nearby suburban communities and the capital city of Berlin with its suburban fringe, which is located in the land of Brandenburg. The massive suburbanization of Berlin is also the most relevant factor for Brandenburg having a positive balance of migration since 1990 (Figures 24 & 25). This also means that only a very limited number of Brandenburg's towns and cities really did experience population growth by migration. Berlin plays a key role: if Berlin was counted as a part of the Neue Länder, the recent positive balance would vanish.

Figure 24: Circular flow chart of dominating internal migration between German Länder 1991-2015

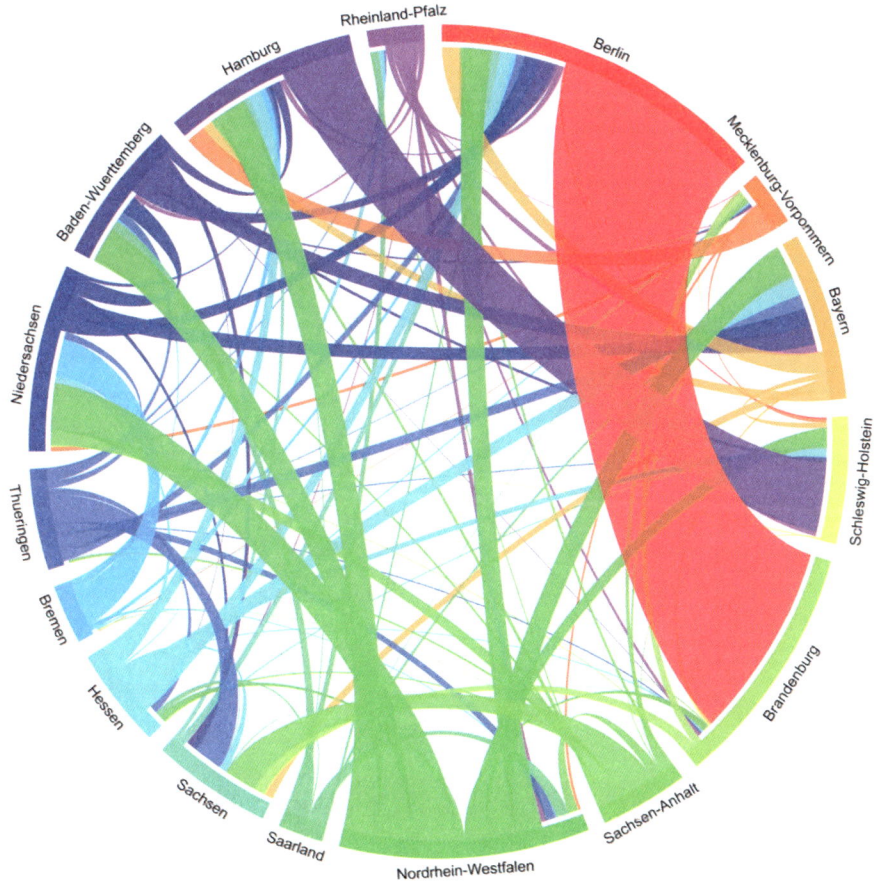

Source: Statistisches Bundesamt 2017

Figure 25: Internal migration of German Länder per 10,000 of population 1991-2015

Percentage (%)

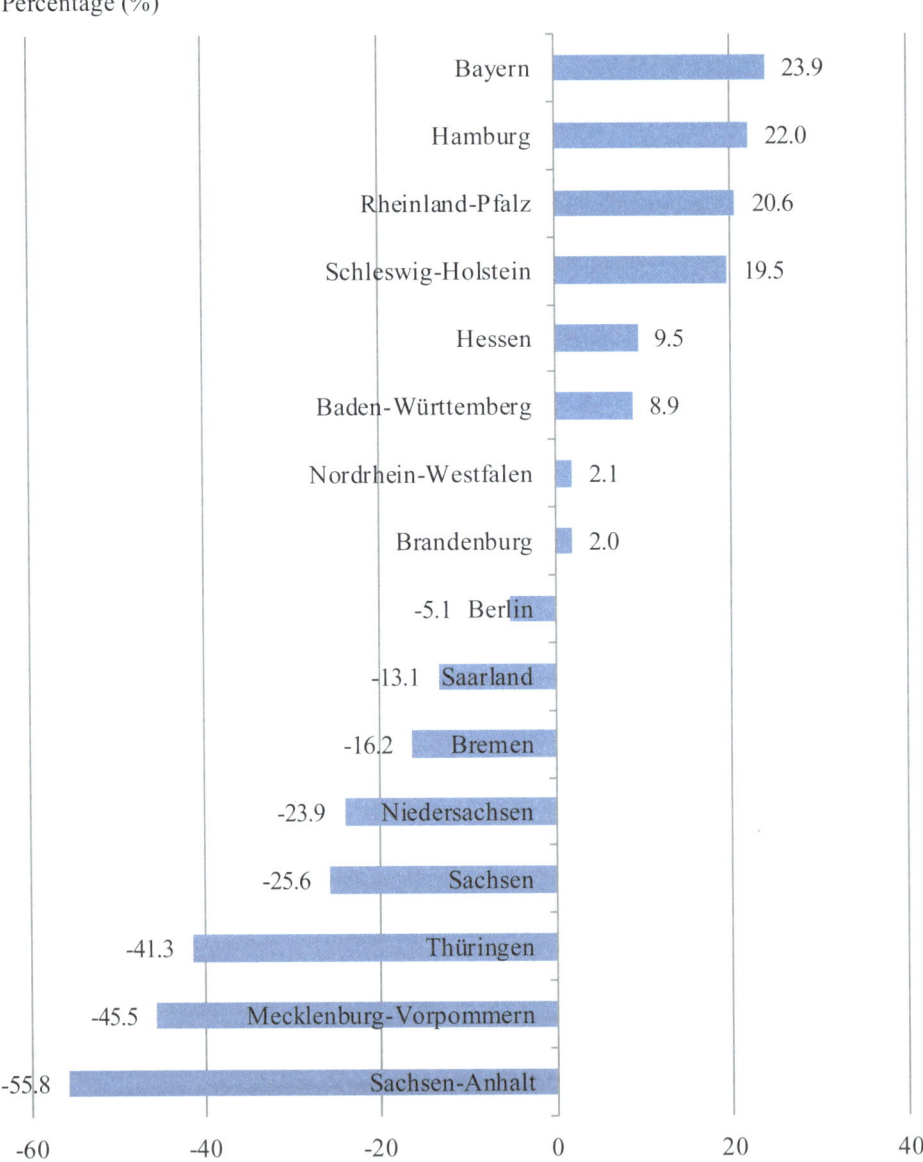

Source: Statistisches Bundesamt 2017

Suburbanization and the very recent "back to the city" trend is the other major feature dominating internal migration in Germany, as can be seen by the high number of migrants from the small city-states of Hamburg, Bremen and certainly Berlin with their neighboring Länder. Also, the relatively high volume of migration between Sachsen and Sachsen Anhalt is related to "cross-Länder border" suburbanization processes of Leipzig and Halle, two cities located very close to the border of Länder (Figure 24).

Hence, the reversal of the trend of German internal migration is not very stable yet. Finally, negative internal migration is still the dominating characteristic for the Neue Länder and this situation has only changed for about one-third of towns in the last three years.

This gradual replacement of the rather uniform east-west direction of Germany's internal migration by a more or less even balance and more diverse patterns within the Neue Länder was recently analyzed (Berlin-Institut für Bevölkerung und Entwicklung 2016). As mentioned above, it is mainly the big cities, the capital city of Berlin and selected suburban towns that experience population increases due to steady immigration from peripheral towns in the Neue Länder and the Alte Länder in general. Unfortunately, German statistics do not provide information on how many of these west-east migrants are East German-born "re-settlers." West German students seem to play an important role in this context since a significant proportion of these migrants is rather young (aged 20 to 30 years) and heading to well-known university cities such as Leipzig, Jena, Greifswald, Rostock and Dresden. But also lesser-known university towns (Halle, Magdeburg, Chemnitz, etc.) are realizing positive migratory balances due to a younger generation moving to the cities. With regard to the stability of this trend, especially the age structure makes it rather uncertain, as young people tend to be more mobile and a sudden reversal of the current pattern is easily possible.

Also, actual re-urbanization and the reversed migration balance in favor of the Neue Länder must not mislead us to underestimate the role of migration on German demographics. As Mai and Scharein (2009) showed via modelling and ex-post population projection for the period between 1990 and 2004, massive migration out of the Neue Länder significantly changed the population structure. Without selective population losses by migration, in 2004 the birth rate in the Neue Länder would have been 12.3 percent higher and 1.3 percent lower in the Alte Länder. Moreover, ageing would not have been as rapid in the Neue Länder. Thus, internal migration has accelerated ageing and population loss in the Neue Länder to a large extent.

Besides the long-dominant Neue Länder-Alte Länder disparities, there is a less accentuated north-south relationship in internal migration, which is the "other" important migration pattern for Germany on a macro-regional level. Basically, the economic centers in the south of Germany represent attractive job markets and also offer other important infrastructures. In migration theory there are certainly various explanations and predictors for the observed migration of people, of which labor market, housing and real-estate market as well as biographical markers and individual circumstances are the most prominent factors. For the case of Germany after reunification, economic aspects (labor market) and housing (suburbanization/re-urbanization) are of particular dominance (see also Schlömer 2009). Biographical and individual aspects cannot be ignored (especially in the form of family unification, e.g. after one partner moved to the Alte Länder), but are not as important as the two other factors yet.

With the recent decline in east-west migration, the north-south pattern as well as intraregional migration flux and re-urbanization tendencies become more visible and shape the internal migration of Germany. As the Neue Länder's urban network is less dense than in

West Germany (with partial exceptions in the southernmost Neue Länder Thüringen and Sachsen, which have a system of urban clusters) and rural regions of mainly moderate economic dynamics and rather poor infrastructure dominate, rural-urban migration in the sense of rural exodus towards the capital city of Berlin and the major East German cities and their close suburban fringes represents a persistent pattern. This is also true for the decade of massive urban decline in the 1990s, where extreme suburbanization scattered the cities' demographics. It is just that rural-urban migration existing even then "disappeared" in the big picture, which was shaped by general east-west migration and suburbanization of East German cities (Köppen 2005). With "sedated" migration between the Alte and Neue Länder, the urban regional centers emerged as poles of stability and attractiveness in the Neue Länder. Thus, most of migration into and within the Neue Länder is also directed into these centers. The former simple east-west scheme is obsolete for characterizing internal migration in Germany. Since 2002, migration from East to West Germany has been decreasing, while the East German cities, particularly Berlin, Leipzig and Dresden, have increasingly profited from internal migration flows (Sander 2014).

However, for more than two decades since reunification, about two-thirds of East German towns have experienced negative internal migration balances. The current immigration from the Alte to Neue Länder is sharply channeled to university cities, administrative centers (the capital cities of the respective Länder) and business hubs.

Furthermore, inner- and intra-regional migration within the Neue Länder is becoming more important and becomes visible in statistics. The above-mentioned re-urbanization of East German cities as "poles of demographic stability" is almost exclusively based on internal migration from the Alte Länder and the structurally weak East German hinterland. This also means that the renaissance of East German cities is directly connected to accelerated demographic decline and brain drain in the nearby peripheral regions; thus there is an increasing urban-rural-suburban contrast in terms of population structure, migration and also regional development.

For the future, a less accentuated Neue Länder-Alte Länder dominance in internal migration can be expected. Nonetheless, significant disparities still exist and will remain.

2.3.4 International migration

International migration was extremely low, if not almost nonexistent, in the GDR, while it represented (and represents) the major driver of population growth in the FRG with only very short periods of negative balance. Also today, mainly due to poor job opportunities and the partially problematic image of some sub-regions, the Neue Länder are the least attractive part of Germany for international migrants (Figure 26). Thus, in the context of reunification demographics, international migration is an indicator that displays a persistent east-west divide.

Figure 26: International migration balance (%) of German Länder 1991-2015

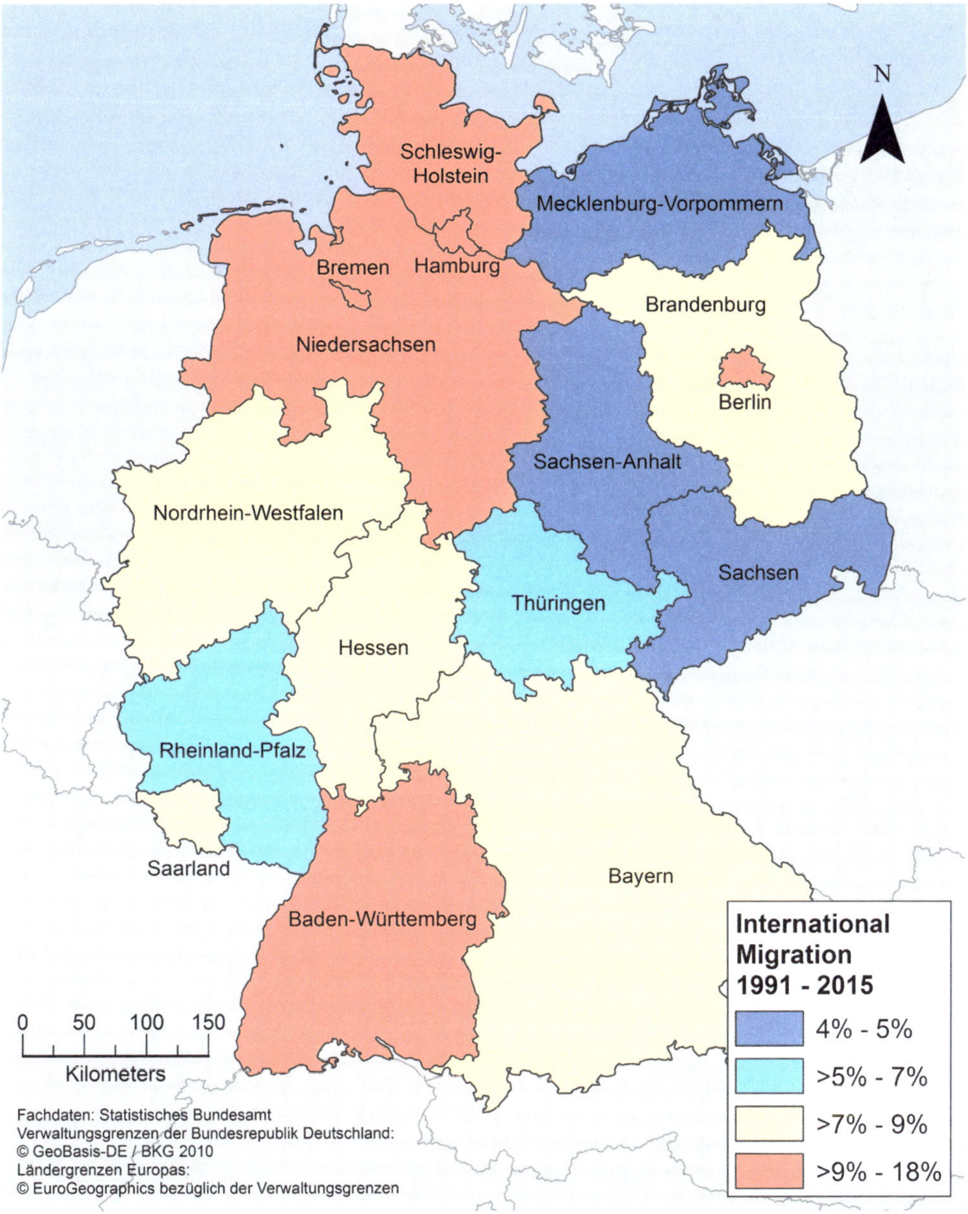

In 2015, out of 16.7 million people with a migration background in Germany, the majority (over 90%) lived in the Alte Länder. Less than 5 percent were living in the Neue Länder. People with migration backgrounds in Germany are all foreigners and naturalized former foreigners, including repatriates of German ethnics, mainly from former Soviet Union and Central Europe, as well Germans with at least one immigrant or foreign-born parent. Thus, this group is larger than just the number of people holding a foreign passport. The long-time presence of foreigners, large numbers of repatriates (about 3.5 million) and naturalized persons is anticipated by this approach in German population statistics.

The foreigners employed as guest workers since 1955 in the FRG mainly settled in industrial conurbations of the southern and western parts of West Germany before 1990. For example, in Nordrhein-Westfalen, the settlements of the population with an immigration background are often the old industrial areas where coal mines and large iron and steel mills as well as related industries (automotive, chemical) used to be. The need for workers exceeded German the workforce at that time. Even today, the economically strong Länder of Baden-Württemberg (28%), Hessen (28%) and Nordrhein-Westfalen (25%) show high rates of persons with migration backgrounds in relation to the total population (Statistische Ämter des Bundes und der Länder, 2015). As a rule, people with migration backgrounds are more likely to live in urban areas and large cities.

In the Neue Länder, on the other hand, the proportions of the population with a migration background were around 5 percent of the total population in 2015 (Figure 27).

With regard to the origin of populations with migration backgrounds there are differences between the Alte and Neue Länder. This is closely linked to the history of the two German states. From the mid-1950s onwards, the FRG had concluded employment agreements for guest workers with countries such as Italy, Spain, Turkey and former Yugoslavia, which were urgently needed for the construction of the FRG's economy. Hence, in most parts of the Alte Länder, Turks constitute the largest group among the population with an immigration background: in Berlin and Bremen it amounts to a quarter, in Nordrhein-Westfalen 22 percent, in Hamburg 19 percent and 17 percent in Baden-Württemberg and Hessen.

On the other hand, fellow citizens of Turkish origin are hardly to be found in the Neue Länder. Foreign workers were also hired in GDR in the 1980s. But they came in smaller numbers and were basically from other socialist countries such as Vietnam, Mozambique, Angola and Poland. These contracted workers were not integrated into GDR society and their families could not follow them to Germany. Furthermore after reunification, most of them had to return to their homelands. The largest group of former GDR immigrants in today's Neue Länder consists of citizens of Vietnamese origin with their family members, some of who joined them in Germany only after reunification, as the families of contract workers were not allowed to move but stayed in the home country. However, the Vietnamese represent the only significant group of foreigners and people with migration backgrounds who are not only visible but also have established modest Neue Länder-related migration networks. Except for the Vietnamese, there are no immigrant communities in the Neue Länder (yet) that are so large in size that immigration networks, chain migration and such may develop.

Figure 27: Share of migrants and descendants of migrants in German Länder (%) in 2015

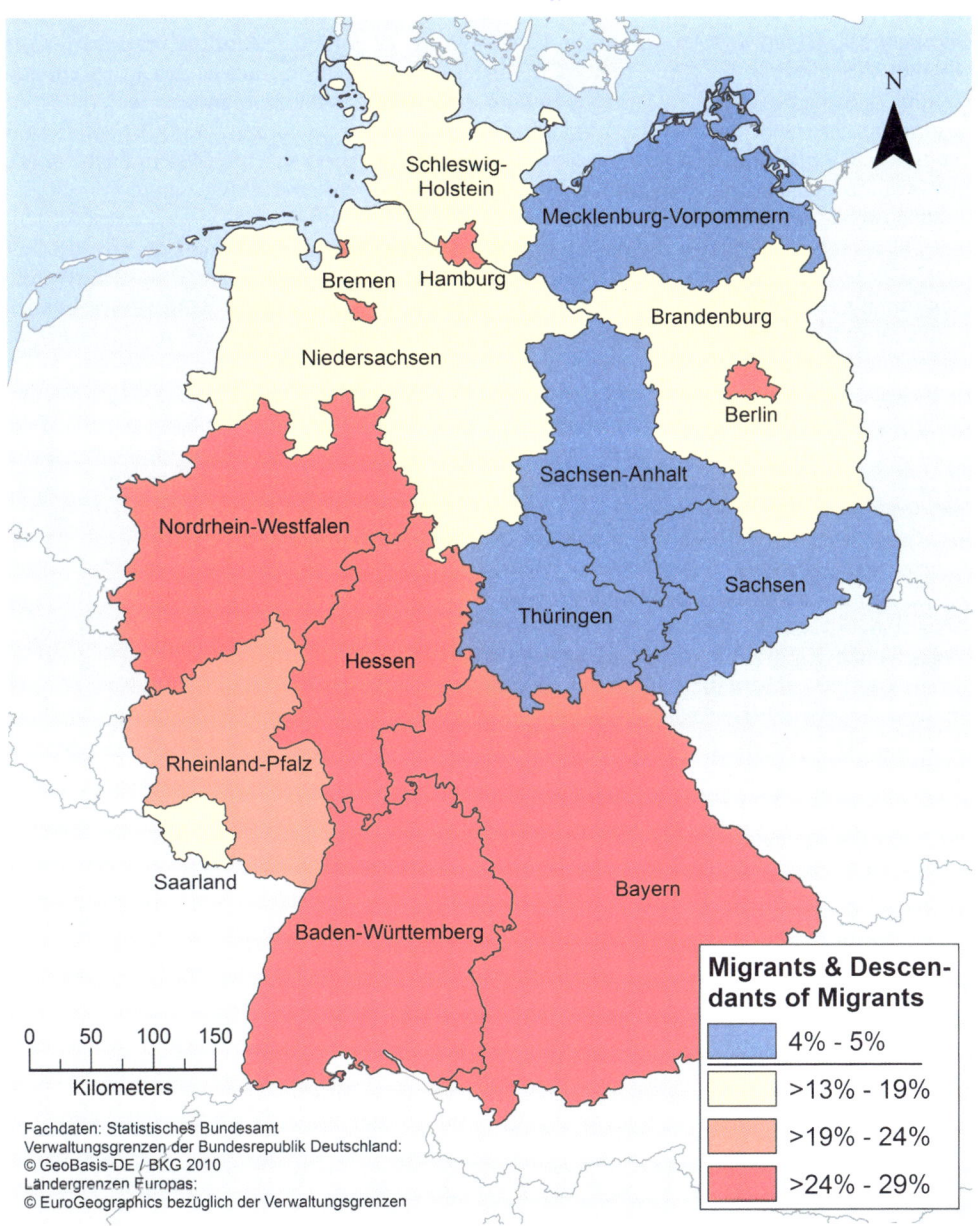

Legend:

Migrants & Descendants of Migrants

- 4% - 5%
- >13% - 19%
- >19% - 24%
- >24% - 29%

Fachdaten: Statistisches Bundesamt
Verwaltungsgrenzen der Bundesrepublik Deutschland:
© GeoBasis-DE / BKG 2010
Ländergrenzen Europas:
© EuroGeographics bezüglich der Verwaltungsgrenzen

The absence of significant immigration in the GDR also meant that most of the people in the Neue Länder were used to living in an ethnically and culturally relatively homogenous environment. Given this fact, there is a lively political, public and scientific debate over whether this specific lack of experience concerning diversity entails a less open society compared to West Germany, where immigration was maybe not always welcome but familiar. In this vein, the outsider's image of the Neue Länder is sometimes associated with xenophobia. This image in combination with the difficult job market does not encourage immigration of foreigners to East Germany (whereas undisputed, fully reliable knowledge on this aspect is not available).

The arrival of about 2 million asylum-seeking refugees in a rather short period between late 2015 and in 2016, when access to Germany was exceptionally granted by the government did a have an immediate impact on the number of foreign citizens in the Neue Länder (as it has for all of the nation). Nonetheless, the long-term consequences are unclear. Asylum seekers in Germany do not have the right to choose their place of residence, but are more or less equally allocated (by a specific allocation system) to all German Länder. Only after being granted asylum in Germany and after having passed a possible hold-off period of up to three years, may these foreigners freely choose their place of domicile. Given the difficult job situation in most parts of the Neue Länder and the presumed xenophobic atmosphere, which is considered to be more accentuated in Eastern Germany, it is rather unlikely that these refugees will stay in the Neue Länder after having the freedom to move and choose their residence.

Hence, although the proportion of foreigners in the Neue Länder today is higher than in 1990, the increase is very low: from around 1.1 percent to around 4 percent in 2015. Neither reunification nor the arrival of refugees has (yet) had a remarkable effect on this. On the contrary, the relative distribution between the numbers in the Neue and Alte Länder prevails in terms of immigrant citizens. As explained above, immigrants tend to avoid the Neue Länder.

3   The socio-cultural and socio-economic perspectives

On the eve of unification, both German states were very different in the light of selected basic indicators related to population and economy (Table 7).

Obviously, the GDR was much smaller than the FRG, in the size of territory and the size of population. Furthermore, there was a major gap in economic performance and the standard of living. Therefore, reunification was not a union of equals in this context.

Table 7: Selected features of FRG and GDR on the eve of reunification

	Federal Republic of Germany 1987	German Democratic Republic 1987
Size of territory	249,000 km²	108,000 km²
Population	61.07 million	16.65 million
TFR	1.43	1.67
Life expectancy	78 (female), 72 (male)	76 (female), 70 (male)
Mortality Rate	11.6 / 1,000	12.9 / 1,000
Immigrants	4,630,218 [7.6%]	191,190 [1.1%] (1989)
GDP	1,065.13 billion EUR	99.34 billion EUR

Source: Statistisches Bundesamt 2017

Also, the political and economic systems were very different (liberal, democratic state with a market economy versus an authoritarian socialist state with closed borders and a command economy), hence the economic situations were very divergent. Actually, the GDR's economy was not going well on the eve of reunification and the 1986 East German GDP was estimated to equal about 9.5 percent of the FRG's GDP. However, the economic figures of both states are very difficult to compare and suitable methods and interpretation are subject to controversial scholarly debate (Ludwig et. al. 2006, Statistisches Bundesamt 2000, Heske 2009).

In the socialist system of the GDR with its planned economy, success and productivity of enterprises were measured based on the Marxist labor theory of value. As a consequence, fair market value was not assessed and thus made it difficult to calculate the assets of the GDR's economy after reunification under the free market paradigm. Hence, a reliable comparison of economic indicators and the standard of living between the GDR and the FRG remains a challenge and reliable data remains sparse (if not unavailable).

To sum up, in political and economic terms, the FRG exhibited better performance and international relevance than the GDR. As for territorial size and population issues, the demographic weight of the FRG also greatly outnumbered that of the GDR. This contrast remains for basic demographics, which have quite different levels and values in both states on the eve of reunification. Cursory examination of selected basic figures suggests structural disparities between east and west, but cannot prove far-reaching cultural alienation of Germans in the decades of separation. In this respect, empirical surveys are needed rather than bulletins and official statistics.

From a political and "technical" viewpoint, formal (state) borders can be changed and broken down quickly and easily. Furthermore, administrative, organizational and economic structures can be rapidly changed by setting a new framework. Borders in people's minds, cultural habits and customs tend to be more stable and lasting.

3.1   Attitudes towards reunification in German society

To commemorate 25 years since reunification, a major survey and comprehensive evaluation of early studies on people's perceptions of the unified nation and their individual positions in society was conducted. The "Deutschland 25" survey (Gabriel et al. 2015) offers a comprehensive insight into German unification from the point of view of German citizens in the Alte and Neue Länder and provides the basis for this chapter on socio-cultural changes and attitudes in reunified Germany.

In turbulent times and in the face of major changes, people often stick to proven and tested strategies in behavior. Therefore, it is seems very unlikely that cultural differences, as they existed between GDR and FRG, would simply disappear from one day to the next. Instead, attitudes change gradually and appear to be path dependent.

When reviewing the changes in social trends and political attitudes in reunified Germany, it is important to understand how political support influences the way people think about a political regime. "Diffuse support" can be defined as a generalized, independent, positive attitude towards basic principles of state political or economic organization. By contrast, "specific support" means the satisfaction with responsible actors, the state political power or economic organization. Although diffuse support often needs time to grow, this does not mean that there is no critical confrontation with the regime. Especially when a growing part of the society is dissatisfied with the political situation, alienation can lead to political resistance, as happened in autumn of 1989 in the GDR. In fact, in 1988, the majority of the GDR population saw themselves as resigned towards the regime, but in 1989 system opponents were growing by up to 40 percent. Starting in 1968, only a minority of East Germans assessed the general living conditions in the country as good or very good and just as many assessed them as very poor. The majority of people considered them average. Moreover, the GDR regime was not able to stabilize the system because of an existing lack of identification among the people with the system. In particular, people criticized the lack of personal freedom, general living conditions and future perspectives. Dissatisfaction also grew because the GDR did not fulfill its own (high) promises to the people to become a societal, cultural and economically leading nation. The regime's credibility was eroded and economic prosperity was no longer given in the late 1980s. This pressure, in combination with rapidly changing geopolitical premises and increasing disconcertment in other European socialist states with Mikhail Gorbachev's doctrine of perestroika as the trailblazer, finally made the GDR a de facto failing state. Soon thereafter, state socialism in all Central European countries was abolished by the people after strong (e.g., the Romanian Revolution of 1989) or little (e.g., the Czechoslovakian Velvet Revolution) resistance to the old regime.

A survey conducted during the process of reunification in March 1990 explored people's opinion in the GDR and FRG about impending German unity. All over Germany, the majority was pleased or very pleased by this perspective and also had similar thoughts about the possible consequences of this historic occurrence.

Between May and August of 1990, an initial representative survey by infratest took place in the GDR. It showed that most GDR citizens were quite optimistic for their future, no matter their age, sex, education, profession or income. Nonetheless, half of the East and West Germans who participated in the survey mentioned some worries, particularly because they deemed reunification was happening too soon and they would have preferred a lengthier process of rapprochement by the two states and societies. Only a small minority were in full opposition to reunification at that time. In July 1990, after the monetary union was the first tangible step to reunification, about 58 percent of East Germans were proponents of unification.

Considering the differences between the two economic systems, it was foreseeable that East German employees would face significant changes in their professional environment that would also require major efforts of adaptation. According to survey data, most people were aware of this and even expected they would lose their job or experience difficulties due to the regime change. Given this awareness, one might suppose that people would prepare for the upcoming challenges and take their fate into their own hands. Actually, this was not observed. Instead, many people waited for the state (government) to intervene and provide solutions, as this was the culture and practice of state socialism. This lack of flexibility led to negative personal consequences and also had an immediate negative impact on the attitude towards the new, reunified nation. The first two years after reunification are known as the economic transformation crisis, with more than 2 million East Germans having lost their jobs. Unsurprisingly, general satisfaction with life decreased during this period. Only one year after reunification, formerly positive attitudes towards democratic, liberal, pluralistic society in general changed dramatically to a very critical view.

However, 1991 marked rock bottom of this development. Since then, satisfaction with life has been increasing, although East Germans remain generally more dissatisfied than West Germans.

Although two different models of society had to be brought together, it is important to note that the FRG's political system was designed as a market economy and conservative welfare state. Thus, even if the two states GDR and FRG were very different states with significant, or even extreme, contrasts in their economic frameworks, political paradigms, human rights etc., East and West Germany had something in common all along: both systems shared the ideal that social welfare should be central concern of the state.

When it comes down to details, such as how far social welfare should reach, East Germans tend to adhere to a more comprehensive understanding as had been promulgated in the socialist GDR. This was not always the case, however. In the very early period of reunification, East Germans considered individual freedom more important than social equilibrium. After having experienced the uncertainties and sometimes the hardships of transformation, the attitude changed and a more socialist welfare state was preferred to the less binding and more fragmentary net of benefits, which accompanied the conservative "West German model" and became reality.

Gender roles in society could not have been more different between GDR and FRG, as described above. While women were a very important factor in the labor force of the GDR, the role model for middle and upper class women in the FRG was different. Staying at home, housekeeping and childcare were considered female duties by a broad swath of the population. In this specific case, the development of role models was very dynamic, moving towards a path of cultural development in Germany as a whole. Since reunification, Germany started a slow but unambiguous process that moved away from the conservative

"West German" idea. Women in the Neue Länder, however, did not fully adapt to the "imported West German" behavior during this time. It is more the west that is gradually adopting the pattern that was predominant in the GDR. This is, however, not an adoption of an eastern norm in West Germany, but a tendency of general modernization and continuing individualization in the Alte Länder's society. The GDR was – quasi coincidently – simply more advanced from today's perspective than the west.

East Germans tend to be more skeptical than West Germans regarding trust in politicians and government politics.

When asking about the individual situation 25 years after reunification compared to the time in the GDR, East Germans tend to rate childcare, social cohesion, social justice and security as well as law enforcement and the quality of education more positively in the GDR than in reunified Germany today (Table 8).

Table 8: Rethinking reunification – Opinions in 2014

		Worse since 1990	Better compared to 1990
Social uplift and career perspectives	Neue Länder		x
	Germany (total)		x
Recognition of individual efforts made	Neue Länder		x
	Germany (total)		x
Social justice and social responsibility	Neue Länder	x	
	Germany (total)	x	
Social security	Neue Länder	x	
	Germany (total)	x	
Protection against crime	Neue Länder	x	
	Germany (total)	x	
Childcare infrastructure	Neue Länder	x	
	Germany (total)		x
Solidarity	Neue Länder	x	
	Germany (total)	x	
Education	Neue Länder	x	
	Germany (total)		x
Healthcare	Neue Länder		x
	Germany (total)	x	
Well-being in society	Neue Länder		x
	Germany (total)		x
Gender equality	Neue Länder		x
	Germany (total)		x

Source: Adapted from Gabriel et al. 2015, p. 136/137

Older East German people in particular share this point of view. However, East Germans younger than 35 years of age see reunification in a much more positive light in all aspects, although also they also tend to point out that social cohesion, childcare and education in the GDR were better than after German unity. This is particularly interesting when considering that these respondents have very little or even no "practical" experience with the GDR system and daily life in state socialism themselves; their "knowledge" is mainly based on what has been passed on from their parents' and grandparents' generations.

It is striking that a similar pattern can be observed in West Germany, although people did not experience a regime change. The younger generation of West Germans thinks that social cohesion and the general situation has improved since 1990, whereas the elder have a more critical perception of post-unification Germany.

The underlying arguments are certainly different: East Germans see critical factors in the system itself, while West Germans are convinced that the positive or negative all-over tendencies are merely a consequence of political practice, thus changeable (Gabriel et al. 2015).

In 1989, when the Iron Curtain fell, the vast majority of East and West Germans was happy and euphoric about the possibility of reunification. Only a small minority was skeptical. Shortly after, the problems of the upcoming process became obvious, resulting in "a wall in the minds," as some people called the many cultural differences between the GDR and FRG. However, to build a democratic community with a stable, powerful democratic order, it is necessary to build it on a foundation of political culture.

In the surveys conducted in autumn of 2014, East and West Germans were asked what parts of Germany they feel most connected to. Both groups determined that they feel the least connected with the part of the other group. In East Germany, the people feel most connected with their place of residence, followed by their county, East Germany, Germany and Europe. Interestingly, the West Germans have another sequence of importance: the county is followed by the place of residence, Germany, West Germany and Europe. With the exception of the stronger connection of East Germans to East Germany than West Germans' connection to West Germany no significant differences exist. The existing differences can be explained by a generation effect that will weaken over time.

However, a current analysis of the "socio-economic panel" (SOEP) for Germany proved that Germans show a very high level of happiness and satisfaction with life. East Germany has reached the highest level since unification in this respect and convergence with West Germany concerning this indicator is almost a given (http://www.zeit.de/2017/24/zufriedenheit-ostdeutschland-juergen-schupp-forscher).

Finally, four out of five East and West Germans see reunification as beneficial for Germany as a whole. Also, East and West Germans agree that East Germany has had more advantages since reunification (Table 9 & Table 10). Hence, Germans seem to generally positively identify with German reunification.

Table 9: Attitudes concerning German reunification in March of 1990 (%)

	Alte Länder	Neue Länder
Very pleased	18.9	40.9
Happy	55.2	50.1
Unhappy	11.9	5.6
Indifferent	13.9	3.3

Source: Adapted from Gabriel et al. 2015, p. 62

Table 10: Reunification: Benefit or disadvantage for Germany? Survey 2014 (%)

	Alte Länder	Neue Länder
Disadvantage	15	12
Undecided/neither-nor	4	7
Benefit	79	80

Source: Adapted from Gabriel et al. 2015, p. 139

3.2   The socio-economic divide – a long lasting challenge

The "state of reunification" is addressed regularly in the *Jahresbericht der Bundesregierung zum Stand der deutschen Einheit* (Federal Government Annual Report on the State of German Reunification). This comprehensive digest of social and economic aspects of living conditions, socio-culture and economic performance in the Neue Länder compared to Alte Länder is a brief assessment of what has been achieved since 1991 and compared to the preceding years. It is not a systematic assessment, however, but tends to cover changing key aspects. The government's vision for Germany is that of a nation with similar living conditions in all regions. Therefore, regional disparities are studied very carefully and strategies for overcoming imbalances are developed. As for the Neue Länder, more than 25 years after reunification, the 2017 Annual Report states that despite impressive advances since 1990, a significant socio-economic divide between East and West remains. Furthermore, it is still not foreseeable when full cohesion will be attained or, as the report puts it, "there is still a long way to go" (Jahresbericht der Bundesregierung zum Stand der deutschen Einheit 2017, p. 9). However, this critical estimate should not mislead us to judge German reunification as a failure. On the contrary, the benchmark by the German government is extremely high and not even matched within the Alte Länder. Similar living conditions in all regions is the central paradigm of German regional policy and spatial planning but cannot be taken literally to the full extent. The key aspect is the provision of basic utilities to the citizens and, in a second step, to further harmonize disparities between regions and compared to the national average. Hence, more or less accentuated disparities are unavoidable; what is seen as problematic, however, are deep, systematic and extensive imbalances. Disparities existed at the moment of reunification for the Neue Länder and significant imbalances still remain today, though they are less accentuated than in 1990.

German division into two different political and economic systems, of which the Federal Republic of Germany finally proved to be the more attractive and successful, created a challenging situation for the Neue Länder after reunification. Most sectors of the East German economy were not really competitive on a global market and (re-)privatization became a more problematic issue than expected (Schröder 2010). Furthermore, public and private infrastructures were far from the standards in the Alte Länder. This imbalance was anticipated by the German government by the very costly and ambitious "Aufbau Ost" (literally Re-building the East) strategy. Aufbau Ost is a general term for all economic and political efforts that were made (and are still in place) to level the Neue and Alte Länder in terms of general living conditions.

Yet the exact costs of reunification remain unclear and are subject to political and scientific discussion. The most commonly agreed estimates of financial transfers to the Neue Länder range between 3.4 trillion euros (an estimate by ifo-Institut Dresden) and 1.5 trillion euros (estimates by Martin-Luther-Universität Halle and Deutsches Institut für Wirtschaftsforschung) for the first 25 years since the GDR joined the FRG (Bundeszentrale für politische Bildung 2015).

It is at least common sense to say that the achievements made in the alignment of socio-economic conditions between the Neue and Alte Länder are impressive although significant gaps remain, as will be illustrated by selected indicators below.

Labor market and unemployment-related data are common indicators for measuring regional economic and social disparities. One major challenge for the Neue Länder until today is a relative lack of major enterprises or big business on an international scale (Bundesamt für Bauwesen und Raumordnung 2012). The same applies to job opportunities with attractive, competitive pay scales (Fink & Jacobs 2014, 32): they are rather rare in the Neue Länder. The female employment rate, however, is significantly higher in the Neue Länder than in West Germany, also as a result of the above-mentioned GDR conventions, whereby women as full members of the workforce were considered a marker of gender equality and also objectively needed. Despite rather rapid economic catching-up in the first years after reunification, today a productivity gap remains (the Neue Länder's productivity is estimated at about 80 percent of the Alte Länder's level) and the gap in the labor market even remains relatively larger (Raumordnungsbericht 2011, Fink & Jacobs 2014, Jahresbericht der Bundesregierung zu deutschen Einheit 2017).

This economic divide can be illustrated by the different level of GDP per person, which shows a rapid increase from 1991 to 2005 for the Neue Länder and relative slow development since then. The gap between both entities became smaller but still remains significant (Table 11).

Table 11: GDP at current prices per person Alte Länder-Neue Länder 1991-2015

	Alte Länder (€)	Neue Länder (€)
1991	22,687	9,701
1995	25,206	16,645
2000	27,959	18,539
2005	30,226	20,660
2010	34,059	24,382
2011	35,707	25,441
2012	36,348	25,970
2013	37,104	26,670
2014	38,187	27,618
2015	39,187	28,702

Source: Jahresbericht der Bundesregierung zum Stand der deutschen Einheit 2017

Below-national-average economic performance (still) remains an unfavorable characteristic of almost all of Neue Länder (Raumordnungsbericht 2011), as the GDP on Länder level clearly shows (Figure 28).

One labor market-related indicator is the unemployment rate, which is also interesting from a demographic point of view: in general, regions with low numbers of unemployed people tend to have a more performant, capacious labor market than regions with high unemployment. Thus, the latter are more likely to be regions of emigration by the skilled workforce, while the other regions tend to attract younger immigrants in particular (Raumordnungsbericht 2011). However, this selective migration of the younger and skilled workers retroacts on the less performant regions, where fewer skilled people remain and a statistical increase in the unemployment rate occurs.

The massive change in the Neue Länder's economic structure produced an immediate loss of workplaces and an increase in unemployment. Despite a successive decrease in unemployment and the current "rise" of economically stable, increasingly attractive urban cores such as the cities of Leipzig and Dresden, the Neue Länder are characterized by high rates of unemployment (Table 12).

Figure 28: Average GDP per person in German Länder 2015

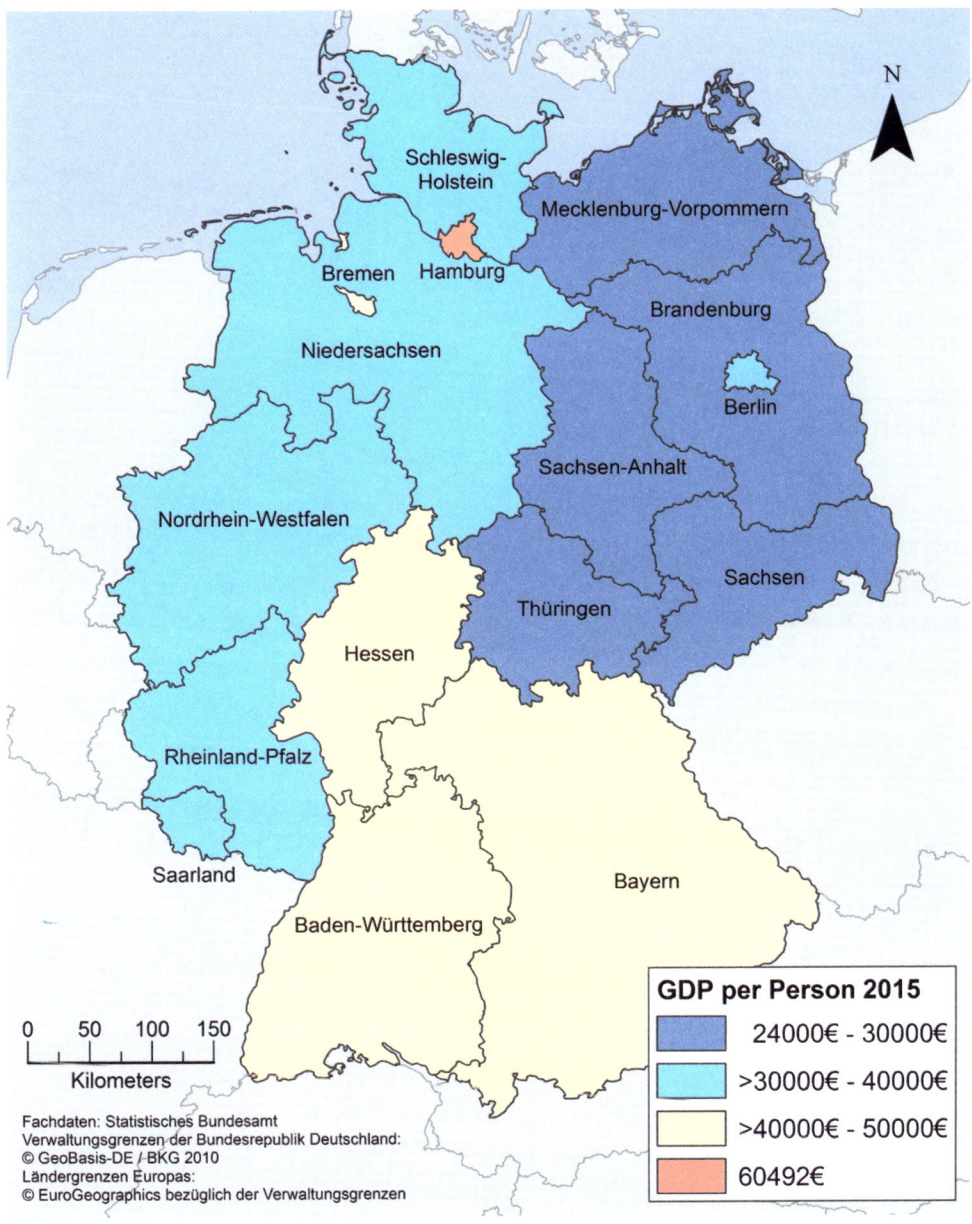

Table 12: Unemployment rate (%) of all civilian workforce not including self-employed
persons 1991-2015 in German Länder

	1991	1992	1993	1994	1995
Baden-Württemberg	3.7	4.4	6.3	7.5	7.4
Bayern	4.4	4.9	6.4	7.1	7.0
Bremen	10.7	10.7	12.4	13.7	14.0
Hamburg	8.7	7.9	8.6	9.8	10.7
Hessen	5.1	5.5	7.0	8.2	8.4
Niedersachsen	8.1	8.1	9.7	10.7	10.9
Nordrhein-Westfalen	7.9	8.0	9.6	10.7	10.6
Rheinland-Pfalz	5.4	5.7	7.5	8.4	8.5
Saarland	8.6	9.0	11.2	12.1	11.7
Schleswig-Holstein	7.3	7.2	8.3	9.0	9.1
Berlin	10.6	12.4	12.8	13.2	13.6
Brandenburg	10.3	14.8	15.3	15.3	14.2
Mecklenburg-Vorpommern	12.5	16.8	17.5	17.0	16.1
Sachsen	9.1	13.6	14.9	15.7	14.4
Sachsen-Anhalt	10.3	15.3	17.2	17.6	16.5
Thüringen	10.2	15.4	16.3	16.5	15.0
	1996	1997	1998	1999	2000
Baden-Württemberg	8.0	8.7	8.0	7.3	6.0
Bayern	7.9	8.7	8.1	7.4	6.3
Bremen	15.6	16.8	16.6	15.7	14.3
Hamburg	11.7	13.0	12.7	11.7	10.0
Hessen	9.3	10.4	10.0	9.4	8.1
Niedersachsen	12.1	12.9	12.3	11.5	10.3
Nordrhein-Westfalen	11.4	12.2	11.7	11.2	10.1
Rheinland-Pfalz	9.4	10.3	9.7	9.2	8.1
Saarland	12.4	13.6	12.6	11.9	10.8
Schleswig-Holstein	10.0	11.2	11.2	10.6	9.5
Berlin	15.2	17.3	17.9	17.7	17.6
Brandenburg	16.2	18.9	18.8	18.7	18.4
Mecklenburg-Vorpommern	18.0	20.3	20.5	19.4	19.0
Sachsen	15.9	18.4	18.8	18.6	18.5
Sachsen-Anhalt	18.8	21.7	21.7	21.7	21.4
Thüringen	16.7	19.1	18.3	16.5	16.5

↓

Table 12: Unemployment rate (%) of all civilian workforce not including self-employed persons 1991-2015 in German Länder – continued

	2001	2002	2003	2004	2005
Baden-Württemberg	5.5	6.1	6.9	6.9	7.8
Bayern	6.0	6.9	7.9	7.9	8.9
Bremen	13.5	13.7	14.4	14.4	18.4
Hamburg	9.3	10.2	11.3	11.0	12.9
Hessen	7.4	7.8	8.8	9.1	10.9
Niedersachsen	10.0	10.2	10.7	10.6	13.0
Nordrhein-Westfalen	9.6	10.1	10.9	11.2	13.2
Rheinland-Pfalz	7.6	8.0	8.5	8.6	9.9
Saarland	9.8	9.9	10.4	10.0	11.7
Schleswig-Holstein	9.4	9.8	10.9	11.1	13.0
Berlin	17.9	18.9	20.2	19.9	21.5
Brandenburg	18.8	19.1	20.4	20.3	19.9
Mecklenburg-Vorpommern	19.6	20.0	21.7	22.1	22.1
Sachsen	19.0	19.3	19.4	19.4	20.0
Sachsen-Anhalt	20.9	20.9	21.8	21.7	21.7
Thüringen	16.5	17.2	18.1	18.1	18.6
	2006	2007	2008	2009	2010
Baden-Württemberg	7.1	5.5	4.6	5.7	5.4
Bayern	7.8	6.1	4.8	5.5	5.1
Bremen	16.3	13.9	12.5	13.0	13.2
Hamburg	12.6	10.5	9.4	10.0	9.5
Hessen	10.4	8.5	7.4	7.6	7.2
Niedersachsen	11.8	9.8	8.5	8.6	8.3
Nordrhein-Westfalen	12.6	10.5	9.3	9.9	9.6
Rheinland-Pfalz	9.0	7.3	6.3	6.8	6.4
Saarland	10.8	9.2	8.0	8.4	8.2
Schleswig-Holstein	11.3	9.5	8.6	8.8	8.5
Berlin	20.1	17.9	16.1	16.4	15.8
Brandenburg	18.7	16.4	14.4	13.6	12.4
Mecklenburg-Vorpommern	20.8	18.1	15.5	14.9	14.0
Sachsen	18.8	16.3	14.3	14.3	13.1
Sachsen-Anhalt	19.9	17.4	15.2	14.8	13.5
Thüringen	17.0	14.4	12.3	12.6	10.9

↓

Table 12: Unemployment rate (%) of all civilian workforce not including self-employed persons 1991-2015 in German Länder – continued

	2011	2012	2013	2014	2015
Baden-Württemberg	4.5	4.4	4.5	4.4	4.3
Bayern	4.3	4.2	4.4	4.3	4.1
Bremen	12.7	12.3	12.3	12.2	12.1
Hamburg	9.0	8.6	8.6	8.7	8.5
Hessen	6.6	6.4	6.6	6.5	6.1
Niedersachsen	7.6	7.3	7.3	7.2	6.8
Nordrhein-Westfalen	8.9	8.9	9.2	9.1	8.8
Rheinland-Pfalz	5.9	5.9	6.1	6.0	5.8
Saarland	7.4	7.3	7.9	7.8	7.7
Schleswig-Holstein	8.2	7.7	7.8	7.6	7.3
Berlin	15.5	14.5	13.9	13.2	12.6
Brandenburg	11.9	11.3	11.0	10.5	9.7
Mecklenburg-Vorpommern	13.8	13.2	12.9	12.2	11.3
Sachsen	11.8	10.9	10.5	9.9	9.2
Sachsen-Anhalt	12.5	12.4	12.1	11.6	11.1
Thüringen	9.8	9.4	9.1	8.6	8.2

Source: Statistisches Bundesamt 2017

The gap between the Alte and Neue Länder remains accentuated even though general unemployment in the Neue Länder has decreased within the last 10 years in particular. Interestingly the global economic crisis of 2008 did not really affect the unemployment rates in Germany and the decrease in the Neue Länder even continued. This decrease is based on several factors. Besides economic stabilization and the formation of the above-mentioned urban poles, east-west migration eased the pressure of job seekers on the Neue Länder's job market. Furthermore, commuting to attractive and broad labor markets in West Germany are especially important for inner-German "border regions." Finally, due to rapid demographic ageing, the sheer numbers of the potential labor force are decreasing. Older unemployed people become retirees and are removed from the unemployment statistics as well as the labor market (Fink & Jacobs 2014).

Also, Alte Länder such as Bremen, Nordrhein-Westfalen and the Saarland (mainly comprising sub-regions shaped by old industries and structural change) show relatively high rates of unemployment, but for every year since reunification, the Neue Länder constantly are notable for above-national-average figures.

The more difficult job situation with lower wages also becomes evident in the average disposable income per person. The common pattern of rapid increase after reunification and slow but steady augmentation with a persistent gap compared to the Alte Länder is also obvious for this aspect of socio-economic development (Table 13).

Table 13: Average disposable income per person (average amount of money per person disposable for consumption and savings per year)

	Alte Länder (€)	Neue Länder (€)
1991	13,788	8,352
1995	15,317	12,175
2000	16,598	13,564
2005	18,546	15,100
2010	20,101	16,836
2011	20,719	17,264
2012	21,201	17,589
2013	21,448	17,854
2014	21,849	18,133
2015	22,312	18,603

Source: Jahresbericht der Bundesregierung zum Stand der deutschen Einheit 2017

More than two decades after the fall of the Iron Curtain and catching up by the Neue Länder, clear differences between East and West are evident in wealth and income. To a certain extent, lower wages and income in the Neue Länder are compensated by lower prices and lower costs of living, but this difference is not sufficient to create relative convergence (Raumordnungsbericht 2011). On average, citizens in the Neue Länder are less affluent than in the Alte Länder.

The German Federal Statistical Office (Statistisches Bundesamt) carries out regular surveys on individual living conditions and the average durable goods in households (Table 14).

With regards to consumer goods and consumption patterns, no evident – or only a minor – gap between East and West remains, however people in the Neue Länder are more price sensitive than in the Alte Länder, which is due to the relatively lower monthly income per person. The relative purchasing power of East Germans is about 87 percent of the West German level (Fink & Jacobs 2014). Nonetheless, in this aspect of socio-economic well-being, Neue and Alte Länder have advanced significantly and although full convergence has not been achieved it is better than for most other indicators. It is also evident that before reunification, the average consumer goods and consumption situation was far less favorable in the Neue Länder than soon after reunification and the dynamics in this sphere are especially high.

Soon after reunification, expectations were very high that the Neue Länder would rapidly and smoothly catch up with the Alte Länder with regard to similar living conditions. The twentieth anniversary of German unity was partially overshadowed by a certain degree of disappointment in the public discourse (Lehman, Ragnitz & May 2010).

Furthermore, negative memories tend to fade and a sort of trivializing GDR nostalgia, "Ostalgie" (literally "Eastalgia"), emerged among some social groups in the Neue Länder. This nostalgia may be related to different factors such as lost social status or unemployment that accompanied reunification, but are also of a psychological nature. Older people in general often tend to feel a positive nostalgia for their memories of young adulthood (Ahbe & Hofmann 2002) regardless of the actual objective conditions at that time.

Table 14: Goods in average German households – Selected items per 100 households

		1993	1998	2003	2008	2013
Alte Länder	Automobile - new	38	37	35	32	34
	Automobile - second hand	41	45	48	51	51
	Dishwasher	38	49	59	64	70
	Dryer	24	33	40	42	44
	Mobile telephone	-	11	73	86	93
	Telephone	97	98	99	99	100
	Washing machine	88	91	93	-	94
Neue Länder	Automobile - new	32	37	34	30	30
	Automobile - second hand	38	40	44	48	44
	Dishwasher	3	26	46	55	59
	Dryer	2	14	20	22	22
	Mobile telephone	-	11	70	86	93
	Telephone	49	96	98	99	100
	Washing machine	91	94	95	-	96

Source: Statistisches Bundesamt 2017

Even today, the job market and economic performance in the Neue Länder are not fully satisfactory in light of the ambitions for successful reunification. However, this "disappointment" completely disremembers the conditions of life and the economic situation in GDR just before the peaceful revolution and the fall of the Iron Curtain. The system change in GDR was obtained in a courageous and unprecedentedly peaceful way by the citizens because of their deep dissatisfaction with the oppressive, authoritarian regime, but also the relatively modest living and economic conditions and pollution. The socio-economic conditions have definitively changed for the better for most people in the Neue Länder. However, compared to Alte Länder, the Neue Länder are still falling behind and as memories of meager everyday life in the GDR fade, the achievements made since 1990 sometimes remain underestimated.

In socio-economic as well in cultural terms, reunification is a highly demanding venture, especially for the people of the Neue Länder. In order to achieve and guarantee well-being, social cohesion and successive coalescence, the German government and people made immense political and financial efforts. As a result, the first 10 to 15 years after reunification were characterized by a very dynamic approximation of the Neue Länder to the Alte Länder in practically all spheres with the exception of the labor market and old industries. With an increasing time lag, however, this alignment slowed down and differences between the two parts of Germany in socio-economic terms remain persistent. These gaps are partially a heritage of GDR times with very low standards compared to the FRG in 1989, but are also due to more or less favorable regional structures in the Neue Länder, which hinder successful modern economic development. The high proportion of peripheral rural regions compared to urban cores was not only already a challenge in pre-war Germany but also an unsolved concern of the GDR's regional policy and economic planning.

When linking the possible impact of socio-economic change in the Neue Länder to respective demographic development, two main things are evident. Firstly, uncertainty over the future of individuals (namely the risk of unemployment) caused a period of "social freezing" where important decisions, including many of demographic relevance such as childbirth but also divorce or marriage, were postponed by people in the Neue Länder. Secondly, the socio-economic divide between Neue and Alte Länder as well as between East German urban cores and East German peripheral regions has an impact on internal migration patterns. The current socio-economic as well as demographic "take off" in East German major cities, after a period of demographic decline and stagnation, testifies to a more complex pattern, which is not only dominated by the divide between Alte Länder and Neue Länder, but also by intra-regional disparities and uneven development. In this context, the primary challenge in regional socio-economic development for the Neue Länder is not their relative difference to the Alte Länder, but the fact that the East German urban poles' growth is strongly linked to further and accelerated decline in the nearby peripheral and structurally backward regions. The latter regions are one important "source" of skilled, young people who today are not forced to leave their homes for better perspectives in the Alte Länder but also in the re-urbanized, attractive major cities of East Germany. The east-west socio-economic (and also demographic!) divide remains, but is increasingly re-shaped and diluted by intra-regional trends and developments.

4 Consequences of post-unification demographics: A persistent east-west divide? (with Michael Mühlichen, BiB)

The major focus of this study is the impact of reunification on population development and structure, although it is not possible to clearly determine to what extent reunification or other, parallel conditions were the chief shapers of demographic changes since 1990. It has already been mentioned that most development is embedded in long-term trends with temporary oscillating values related to reunification or the specific regulatory system of the authoritarian GDR regime. As an example, the sudden decline in births within a general tendency towards lower fertility and massive outbound migration from the Neue Länder are linked reunification and regional east-west disparities in economic prosperity. They are prototypical "direct" consequences of reunification, shaping the demographic patterns and structure. Current convergence in TFR, however, is associated with the long-term phenomenon of the Second Demographic Transition and the high numbers of babies born out of wedlock in the Neue Länder were rooted in historical periods (and conditions) even before Germany was separated, to give an example.

What is clear is that following the opening of the GDR-FRG border in November of 1989 and reunification on October 3, 1990, the Neue Länder experienced rapid population decline and rapid ageing, mainly due to low birth rates and emigration to the Alte Länder. These phenomena are typical markers of shrinking regions (Maretzke 2009). The immediate post-unification demographic decomposition of the Neue Länder's former population structure is a cornerstone to sustained demographic shrinkage and increasing regional disparities, which are intensified as well as accelerated by low fertility. Hence, as mentioned above, despite today's convergence of the main demographic drivers (TFR, mortality/life expectancy and migration balance), the consequences of demographic disparities between Alte and Neue Länder during the first two decades since reunification will perpetuate and be visible for an unpredictable period in the future.

Low fertility and ageing are probably among the most challenging demographic trends for Germany's future and the division between the Alte and Neue Länder will remain visible for a long time especially in terms of age structure.

Both states, the GDR and FRG, experienced low replacement fertility since the early 1970s. The low fertility level did not affect the FRG's population balance negatively in most years because immigration was higher than emigration most of the time. In the GDR, however, immigration was extremely low, if not almost nonexistent, but pro-natalist social state policy led to a temporary era of increased fertility in the late 1970s and the 1980s, which slightly delayed population decrease. Along with increasing life expectancy, the weakness in births led to a subsequent ageing of society in both states. The average age has almost continuously increased in Germany since the beginning of the 20th century, except for the period of the so-called baby boomers (1960s). At the time of reunification, the East German population was considerably younger than the West German population on average, both men (-1.98 years) and women (-1.55 years) (see Table 15).

Table 15: Average age of men and women in East and West Germany at the end of 1990 and in 2015

	Men		Women	
	1990	2015	1990	2015
Eastern Germany	35.49	44.25	40.12	47.52
Western Germany	37.47	42.46	41.67	45.07
Total	37.08	42.81	41.36	45.61

Source: Statistisches Bundesamt 2017

This was particularly due to the comparatively higher birth rates in the 1970s and 1980s. However, this has changed to the opposite: Whereas the sharp decline in fertility, the strong increase of migration by young people from east to west and the advanced rise in life expectancy following the fall of the Berlin Wall accelerated population ageing in East Germany, the immense migration surplus cushioned population ageing in West Germany. Both men (+1.79 years) and women (+2.45 years) are older now in East Germany.

This diverse development of population ageing becomes clearer when we analyze the different age groups. Thus, the proportion of people aged 45 and older has increased in both parts of Germany since 1990, but to a larger degree in the eastern part. In 2015, the people aged 45 and older made up 50.4 percent in the Alte Länder and even 54.1 percent in the Neue Länder. In 1990, the proportion was only 40.7 percent and 39.2 percent, respectively. Conversely, the proportion of the younger age groups has decreased. The decline in the percentage of people aged 0 to 14 was especially strong in the east between 1990 and 2005. Since then, this age group has showed a slight increase again in the east as a consequence of increased birth rates, which exceeded the West German level in recent years.

On the regional level, we also see this reversal: All German Länder have experienced an increase in average age since 1990, but to a much different degree (Figures 29 & 30). Mecklenburg-Vorpommern had the lowest average age, 35.8 years, of all German Länder in 1990. Since then, it has risen to 46.5 years by 2015. All of the five Neue Länder (excluding Berlin) show older populations now on average than the other Länder. Bayern and Baden-Württemberg in the south have remained relatively young. Only the federal city-states of Hamburg and Berlin now show a lower average age. Hamburg was the "oldest" German state in 1990 with an average age of 41.7 years but became the "youngest" by 2015 with 42.3 years due to an immense migration surplus of young people.

Figure 29: Average age in the German Länder on December 31, 1991

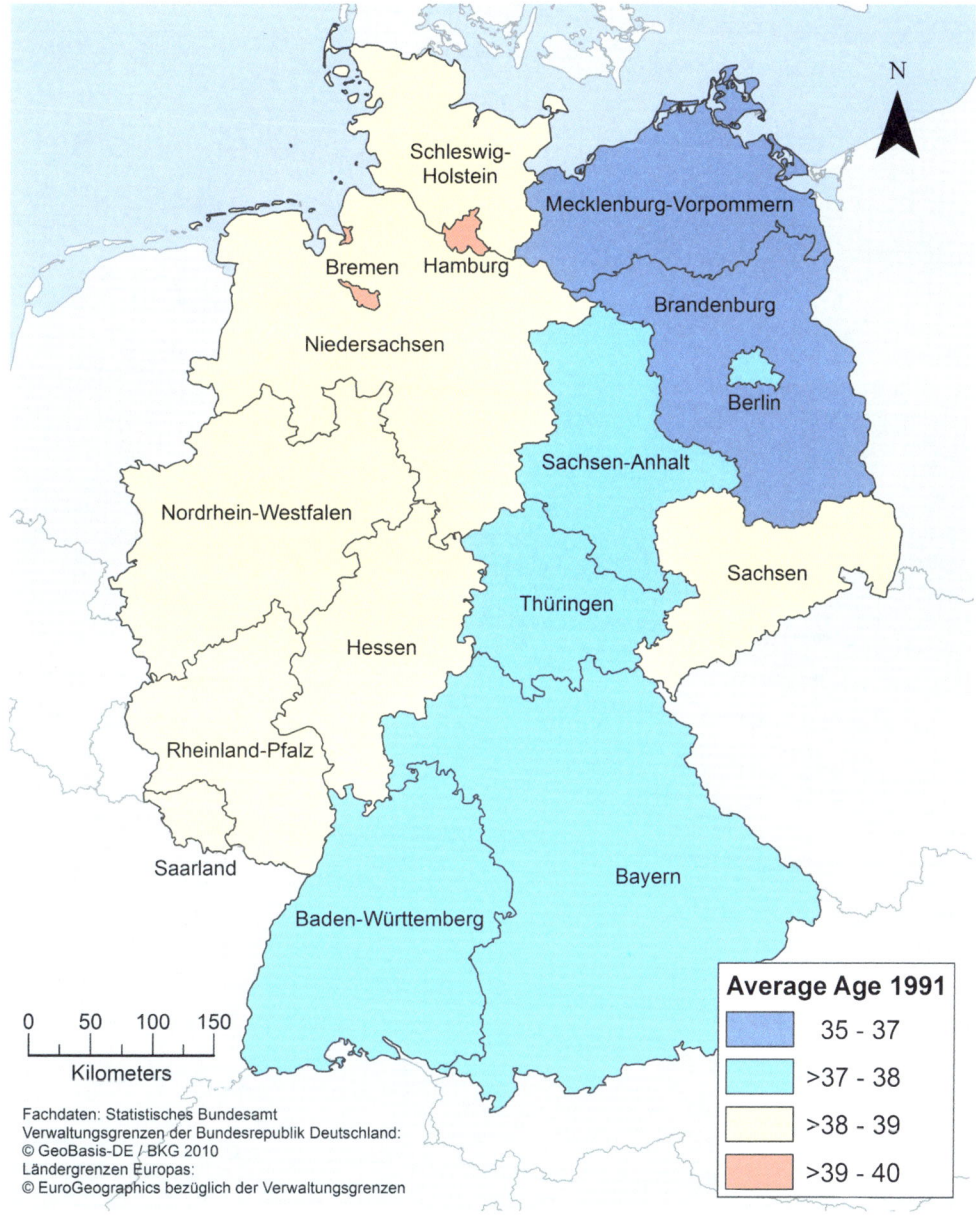

Figure 30: Average age in the German Länder on December 31, 2015

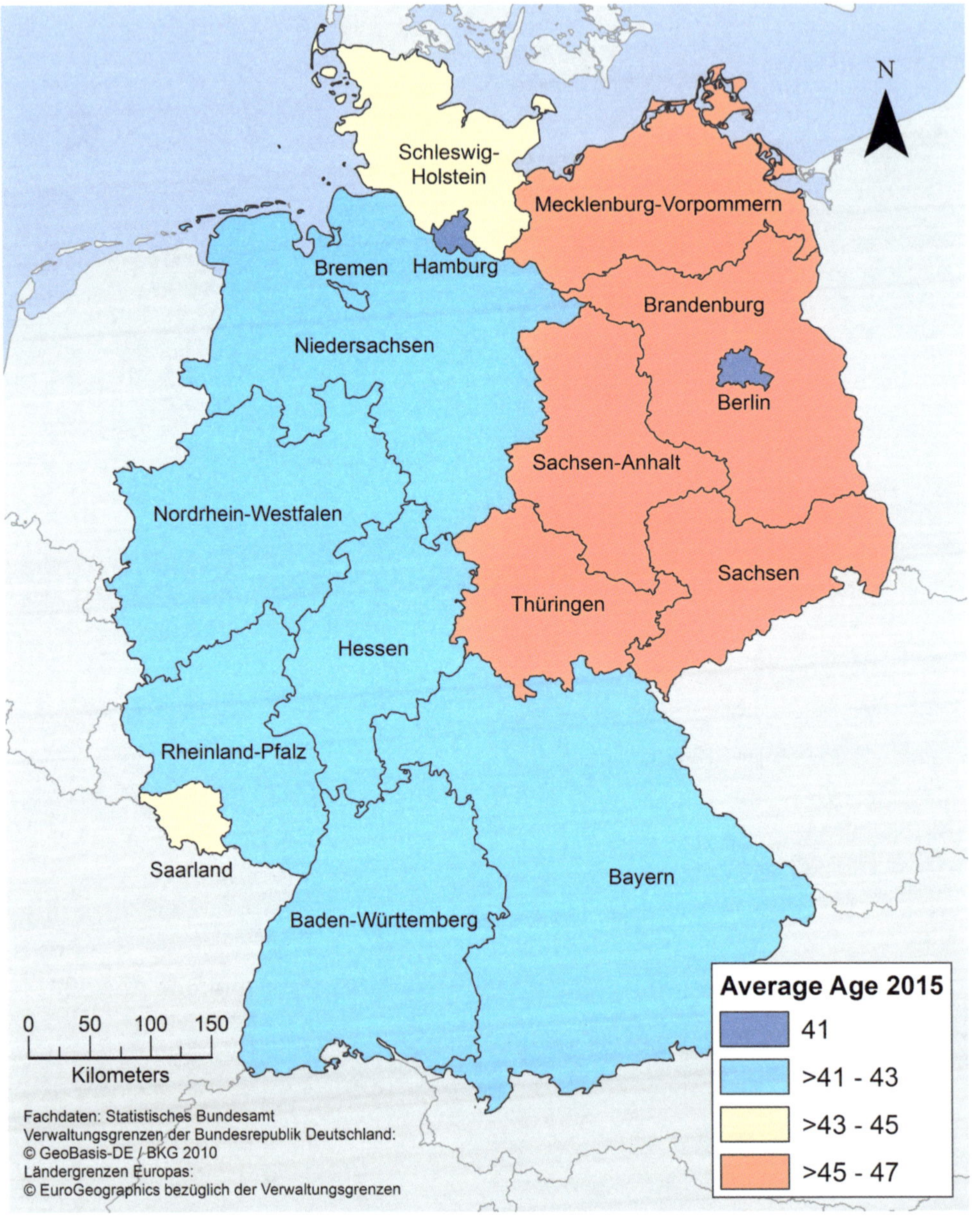

A further tangible and inevitable consequence of ageing is rapid demographic change, marked by a shift in dependency ratios and age structure. Between 1991 and 2015, the proportion of the older population in Germany increased. The old age dependency ratio – the proportion of people 65 years old and older compared to 100 of population aged 20 to 64 years (working age), also increased; especially in the Neue Länder (Table 16), where today, this ratio is significantly higher than the German average.

Table 16: Old-age dependency ratio in the Alte and Neue Länder 1990-2015

	Alte Länder	Neue Länder
1990	23.9	22.4
1991	23.9	22.5
1992	24.0	22.5
1993	24.3	22.8
1994	24.7	23.2
1995	25.1	23.5
1996	25.3	23.8
1997	25.5	24.1
1998	25.7	24.4
1999	26.3	25.1
2000	26.9	26.1
2001	27.6	27.1
2002	28.3	28.2
2003	29.2	29.4
2004	30.4	30.9
2005	31.5	32.4
2006	32.4	33.9
2007	32.8	34.7
2008	33.2	35.6
2009	33.5	36.3
2010	33.2	36.2
2011	33.3	36.6
2012	33.3	36.9
2013	33.5	37.2
2014	33.8	37.9
2015	33.8	38.5

Source: Statistisches Bundesamt 2017

Sachsen and Sachsen-Anhalt have the highest ratios in Germany in this respect. The lowest ratio can be found in the small German Länder Berlin and Hamburg. Since migration to the city is currently shaped by younger migrants, the ratio in cities is generally lower than elsewhere (Statistische Ämter des Bundes und der Länder 2015).

The increasing old age dependency ratio in Germany represents a major challenge for social security and pension funds, as current organization relies to a significant extent on generational solidarity. Thus, an intelligent strategy to maintain the high standards of the German social market economy and welfare systems in an ageing society still needs to be established.

The changes of demographic structure since reunification explained above are especially obvious when comparing the population pyramids of 1990 and 2015 (Figures 31 & 32). Due its higher fertility between the late 1970s and 1990, underage persons had a comparatively higher share in the east in 1990. Older people, however, had a higher proportion in the west due to the east-west gradient in life expectancy that emerged as from the late 1970s and peaked in 1990. Higher mortality in the GDR was particularly distinct at retirement age. After reunification, the gap in life expectancy began to vanish but is still evident among men to a small degree, whereas fertility in East Germany first greatly decreased until 1994 before it normalized and exceeded the West German fertility level again in recent years. Both the strong increase in life expectancy and the drop in fertility, but also the selective emigration of young people from east to west, accelerated the ageing of the East German population. Whereas the Eastern German population was relatively young in comparison to the west in 1990, it became comparatively old by 2015.

Thus, the first decade of the reunified nation finally caused a long-term demographic "deformation" compared to the previous population structure. Even though full convergence is reported for the TFR and the migration system also gradually levels, the consequences will remain visible for decades to come, as the prior drops were too strong to fill the gaps. From a theoretical point of view, we must consider that demographic processes that rely on population structure, once started, tend to be viscous. From a perspective on population and reunification, it does not even really matter whether the demographic patterns 25 years after uniting the two German states have converged, in accordance with modernization theory, or remain diverse, as expected by divergence theory, or whether hybridization is the best description (as it is actually the case). The short term, but extremely accentuated and oscillating changes in fertility and internal migration shape the Neue Länder's German demography. As for West Germany, a degree of rejuvenation can be ascertained although the effects are slightly less important due to the basis effect related to the imbalance in population size between the Alte Länder (approx. 65 million) and the Neue Länder (approx. 17 million).

Figure 31: Age structure in Western and Eastern Germany on December 31, 1990

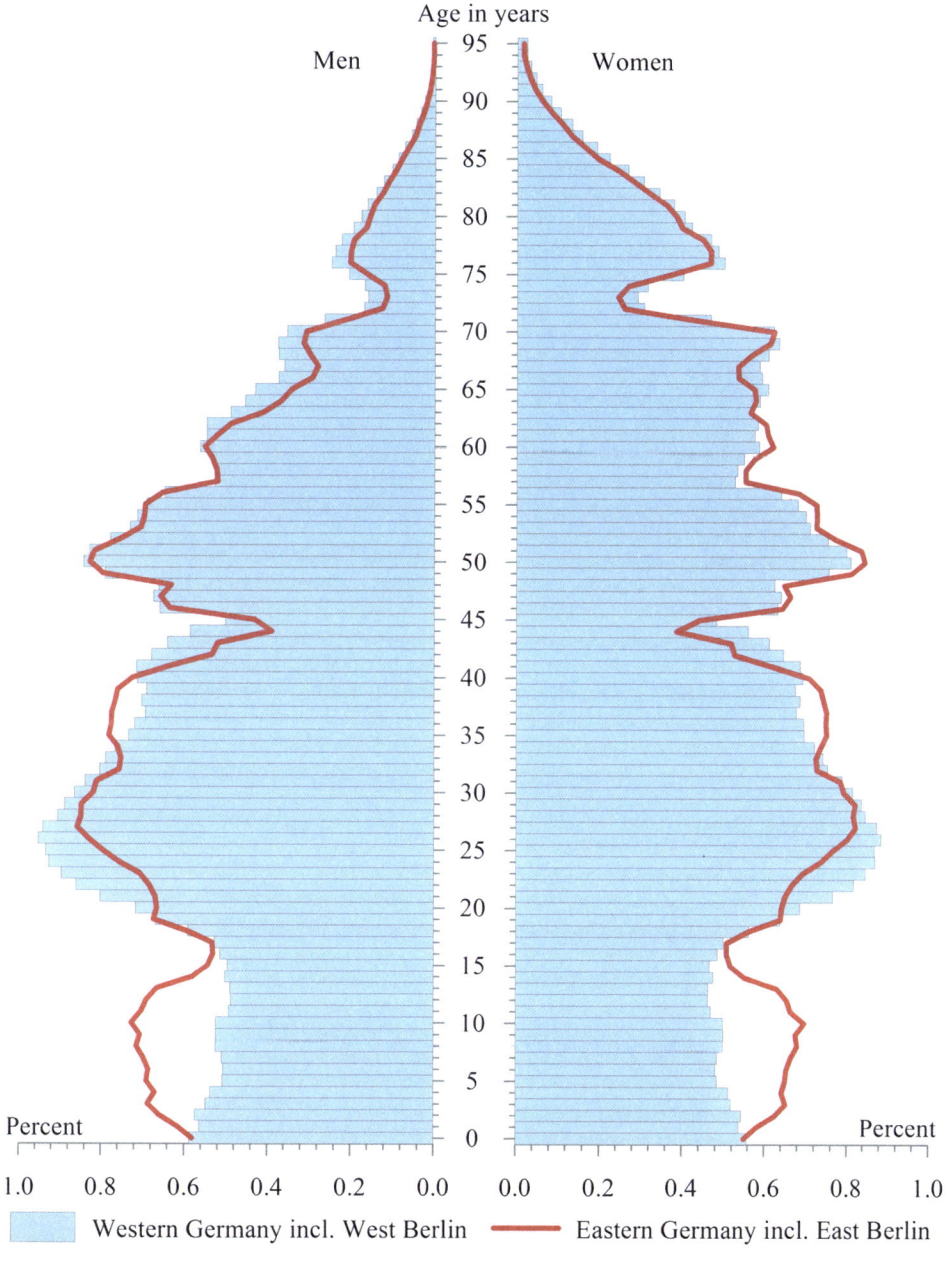

Source: Statistisches Bundesamt 2017

Figure 32: Age structure in Western and Eastern Germany on December 31, 2015

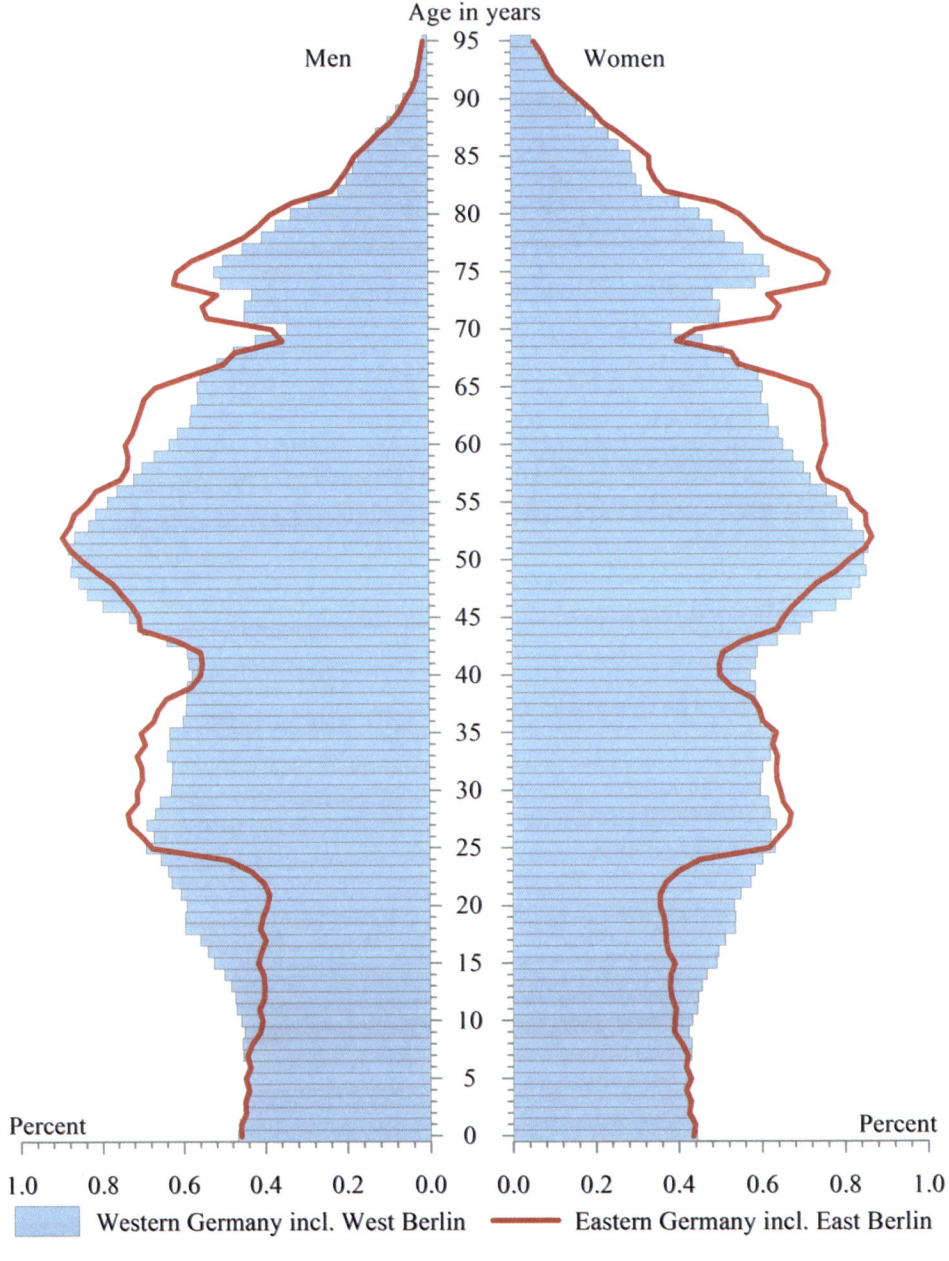

Source: Statistisches Bundesamt 2017

Regarding the sex ratio, both East and West Germany experienced significant changes since the Second World War. The sex ratio, or the number of men per 100 women, is particularly influenced by gender-specific mortality rates and migration streams. Whereas the sex ratio is usually about 105 men per 100 women at birth, this value decreases with rising age because of greater age-specific mortality rates among men compared to women. Average life expectancy has been higher for women since the beginning of official German statistics (Figure 33).

Figure 33: Sex ratio in West and East Germany (East Germany including West Berlin as from 2001) by age 1950–2015

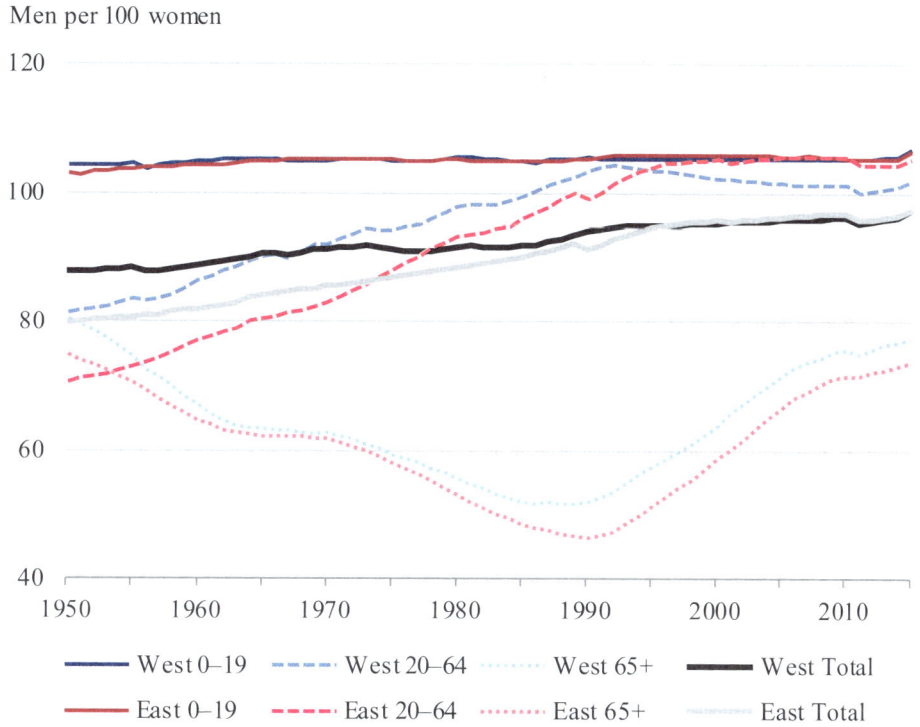

Note: East Germany including West Berlin as from 2001 due to data restrictions
Source: Statistisches Bundesamt 2017

In addition, male cohorts were decimated to a higher extent than women in the World Wars. The influence of the two World Wars on the sex ratio was especially high in the 1950s at middle and older adult ages and to a higher degree in the east than in the west. Meanwhile, this influence is only visible at very old ages. But the gap in life expectancy between men and women grew until the late 1970s and did not start to decline until the mid-1990s. Thus, the mortality gap between the two sexes has a considerable impact on the sex ratio as well, particularly at age 65 and older. Another important factor is migration, thus is related to reunification and its consequences. East Germany has experienced a negative migration balance for most years since the fall of the Wall because more people migrated from east to west than the other way around. This balance is particularly negative among women, not due to higher emigration of women than men, which is not the case, but because considerably fewer women migrate to the east than men (as explained above). Therefore, the sex ratio of the population at working age grew in the 1990s and 2000s in the east, especially in the rural parts, whereas it decreased in the west. In addition, the recent flow of refugees to Germany is dominated by men, which explains the increase of the sex ratio in 2015.

At this point, however, we must state that the exact effects of de- and re-composition of the respective population structures in the Neue and Alte Länder has not been ascertained as it is difficult to estimate. German statistics provide aggregated data and no information on individuals beside the census. The latter, however, is not useful for our information as Germany's last census was sample based and not a full inventory. Studying the local demographic effects of population de- and re-composition by east-west migrations would require a) data on individuals and their migration history as well as b) a full inventory. Furthermore, the underlying cases in the aggregated data do not have distinct identifiers, thus they cannot be linked to case-specific information from another dataset. Under these conditions, even indirect measures do not work or remain very vague.

With 4.5 million people having moved from the Neue Länder to the Alte Länder between 1991 and 2015 (plus those East Germans who left in the short time span between the opening of the border in November of 1989 and 1991), it is clear that those West German cities and regions that became the new home to these inner-German migrants rejuvenated with an increase in population of working age and youth (either as children coming with their parents or babies born to younger East German women after having settled in the Alte Länder). The rough modelling of this effect by Scharein & Mai (2009) has already been mentioned, hence a more detailed model for Germany on county or even communal level would be very interesting, but is almost impossible due to the described restrictions in data availability. Finally, 2.5 million migrants out of a population of initially 16 million is significant, but we must also realize that these migrants integrated in a West German population of roughly 65 million. Thus, their measurable effect on the population structure of the Alte Länder is minimal while their departure leaves an obvious gap in their home region. Thus, the decomposition of the Neue Länder's population by low fertility and emigration is considerable, while the effects in the Alte Länder are positive but rather invisible, especially in a long term perspective.

This demographic "heritage" does have an impact on regional development. Tangible consequences today are mainly the absence of a younger population and an aged society in the Neue Länder. Furthermore, regional disparities within the Neue Länder remain rigid and fixed; significant population growth and potential rejuvenation are fully dependent on immigration. While the Alte Länder-related migration of recent decades also helped to mitigate the problem of unemployment in the Neue Länder, in the near future, the lack of population of working age will become a challenge for all of Germany. A significant lack of skilled people is feared, although we must mention that this expected future shortage of well-trained tradespeople requires a critical review. Actually, Germany has a particularly large rate of female underemployment due to traditional attitudes and inflexible workplace management. Thus, the hidden reserves (non-working skilled women) are high, but remain inactivated as yet.

In the Neue Länder, selective migration of younger and more educated people already decomposed the more favorable structure of population in socio-economical terms since 1990 (Maretzke 2009).

Among the most problematic consequences of accelerated demographic change in the Neue Länder on regional and communal level are the negative impact on public finances and tax revenues and, as a direct consequence, shrinking margins for investments in infrastructure and public service. This in turn weakens relative attractiveness and competitiveness, which might spur a vicious circle with population, enterprises and potential investors fleeing or avoiding these regions and towns.

Currently, demographic stability and growth in the Neue Länder is linked to a few strong urban poles and the capital city of Berlin and its surroundings (Figure 34). Hence, ageing and shrinkage remains a problem for many regions of the Neue Länder.

With reunification, the FRG's framework in all its variations proved quasi-hegemonic for the "new" German nation. Nonetheless, all of Germany also underwent the process of accelerated globalization, like all other advanced societies. Hence, an attempt to measure the state of integration of East Germans and the former GDR into "old" Western Germany/ FRG would be misleading, as the 1990s proved to be an economic and politically turbulent period in which all Western European Societies experienced significant changes compared to the decade before. Thus, citizens of the Neue Länder did not solely adapt to the West German conditions and way of life, but were also confronted with the shift towards a globalizing society. Some authors, like McFalls (1995, 2001), argue that at the core, East Germans adapted even faster to the newly globalized post-unification reality than some West Germans and that the core of societal unification was achieved very quickly.

Then again, others (Klein 2001, Mühlberg 2002) – some with a more distanced view and a less scientific perspective (Decker 2014) – claim that the GDR and FRG developed over the 40 years of division into very different societies also in terms of culture and habits. As a consequence, the cultural difference was much greater than expected at the moment of reunification and "unification in the hearts and minds" remains a long lasting process (Meulemann 2002). What all scholars have in common is that they argue the Western system is "culturally" dominant.

These general findings and our analysis on population development and structure indicate strong convergent tendencies with significant and stable elements of divergence.

Finally, the assumption of hybridization proves adequate when studying Germany's demographic trends since reunification. Despite convergence in terms of internal migration, fertility and mortality as well as life expectancy, divergent patterns also remain. Social practices in both macro regions of Germany (still) differ. In terms of attraction for foreign immigrants, births out of wedlock, labor participation of mothers (and women in general), the Neue Länder stand out and there is no sign of alignment with West German practice or norms. Hence, an east-west divide will remain visible also in a long-term perspective. However, the markers of division are constantly changing and evolving towards modified Neue Länder-Alte Länder divergences. Local and regional differences are becoming more important, gradually making the typical East- or West German less visible, although their basis remains as the underlying foundation. The east-west perspective of the first decade after reunification lost its dominance but prevails now alongside emerging and recurring north-south as well as urban-suburban-rural interdependencies and disparities.

Figure 34: Recent total population development in Germany on the county level 2011–2015

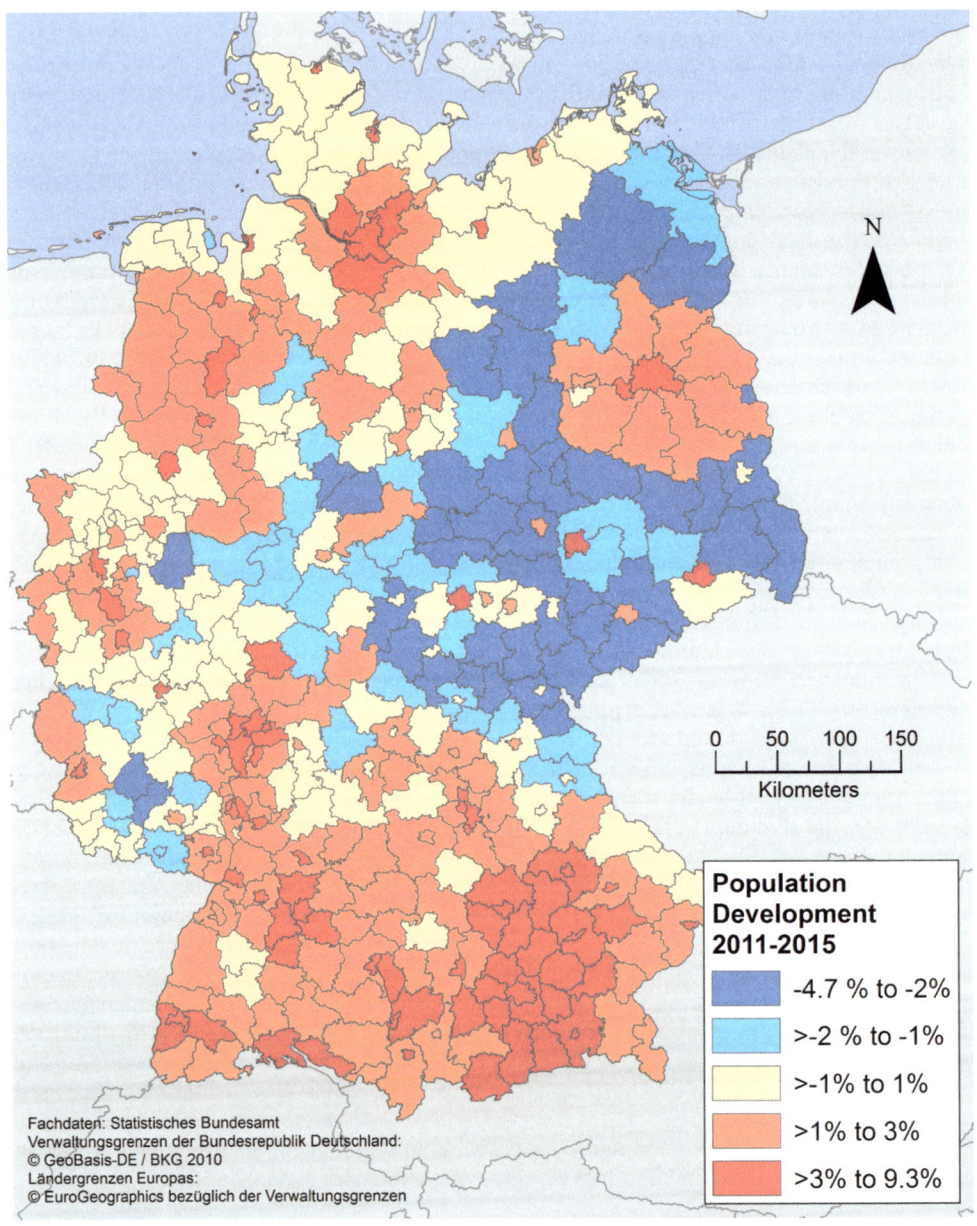

N

0   50   100   150
Kilometers

Population Development 2011-2015

- -4.7 % to -2%
- >-2 % to -1%
- >-1% to 1%
- >1% to 3%
- >3% to 9.3%

Fachdaten: Statistisches Bundesamt
Verwaltungsgrenzen der Bundesrepublik Deutschland:
© GeoBasis-DE / BKG 2010
Ländergrenzen Europas:
© EuroGeographics bezüglich der Verwaltungsgrenzen

5   Knowledge and notions on the demographics of Korean reunification (Sam Hyun Yoo, KIHASA)

The ideal of possible peaceful reunification is part of official, governmental policies in both the Republic of Korea and the Democratic People's Republic of Korea (DPRK). Hence, research and scenarios on reunification are relevant tesserae for inner-Korean policy. The German experience is given special attention in this context as reunification happened fully unexpectedly, suddenly and quickly. Furthermore, like Korea, it was a matter of two distinct political systems in confrontation.

However, many details and general circumstances in Korea are different from those in Germany on the eve of reunification. Compared to the gap between East and West Germany at the time of reunification, South Korea is far more economically advanced than North Korea while North Korea appears to be richer than South Korea in natural resources (Yoon, 2011). The reunification of East and West Germany was closely related to the concomitant geopolitical changes in Central and Eastern Europe (Stephen 2016). For Korea, a similar situation is currently not given. On the contrary, after an attempt at reconciliation and rapprochement between the two states at the turn of the millennium, tensions are very high since Kim Jong Un succeeded his father Kim Jong Il as dictator.

The Korean peninsula is furthermore in the zone of geopolitical attention of four powers: China, Japan, Russia and the United States. Thus, the political impact of a possible Korea reunification is difficult to estimate.

Looking at demographic weight, in 1989, the Federal Republic of Germany (FRG) had a population around four times larger than the German Democratic Republic (GDR) and the leadership and politicians of the East German government were not averse to reunification (Stephen 2016). The same is true for the former allies: despite some doubts, the two German governments were able to conduct the reunification process.

In 2015, South Korea had twice the population of North Korea. The intentions of the political elites in DPRK are nebulous (Klug, 2012). North Korea is essentially a closed society, often described as a "hermit kingdom". As people in North Korea have very little contact with the outside, detailed information about this country is also very limited.

Paying attention to German experience can, nevertheless, provide vital clues for possible changes on the Korean peninsula.

Although North and South Korea have a shared culture, familial ties, history and language, they have been divided for more than six decades. Given the long-lasting separation and political conflicts, a reunification of Korea will most likely bring about challenges in diverse aspects. One of the important challenges would be demographic issues in a reunified Korea.

5.1   Typologies of reunification

Several pathways to system change and reunification are possible, but only a few options are available for the discussion of demographic changes following that reunification or federation of states.

One may consider forced reunification, but this is no more than a worst-case scenario as it would involve violence and war. A military conflict, whether local or full-scale, would very likely devastate both societies, leaving the surviving people with indelible scars.

Immediate damage and causalities after wars might be estimable, but it is rarely possible to gauge demographic changes before and after wars in the journey of this undesirable kind of reunification. As forced reunification by absorption of the DPRK is neither an option, doctrine of South Korean politics nor a constructive strategy with incalculable outcomes, we can exclude this variant of reunification from discussion.

A progressive, gradual reunification in stages of rapprochement and convergence instead appears a feasible and prudent possibility. The idea of gradual reunification is based on transitional phases, which allow gradual adjustment and harmonization of the systems. Problems, frictions and uncertainty would be minimized. Both sides would concentrate on urgent problems in each step before unlocking further levels of integration. This kind of incremental reunification, also in the light of harsh societal and economic disparities between the Republic of Korea and the DPRK, could be a very interesting and feasible strategy.

The third variant would be "German style" reunification: unexpected and sudden. Despite the imperative will of the current regime of North Korea to hold out in its current form, any unexpected change cannot be ruled out. The DPRK experienced recurring natural disasters (including the "Arduous March" famine from 1994 until 1998), is subjected to political isolation, embargo and suffers from economic weakness and mismanagement. Certainly, these problems are directly related to the specific type of political system (Juche/ self reliance and Songun/army first ideology) and the DPRK's geopolitics, but – and this is important – the regime is also under severe permanent stress due to these factors. Hence, an unpredicted sudden change is almost as likely as a long-lasting consolidation of the current situation. It should be noted that German reunification was fully unexpected until it actually happened.

For our scenario, we will consider a sudden and peaceful reunification or a regime change in North Korea moving towards a liberal system with open borders and gradual integration as a basis. In doing so, the German experience can be a reference although the context of reunification is not similar and the extent of reference is very limited.

5.2 Tales of demographic change in an open or reunified Korea

Our scenario for Korea is built in two steps. First, we will develop a largely free vision of Korean reunification and possible consequences for demography with reference to findings from Germany. This part is very progressive, sometimes playful and an exercise in brainstorming. The content, however, will be critically reviewed in the concluding chapter, where only those elements for a Korean scenario remain that are most likely to happen after a regime change in Pyongyang and during eventual reunification on the Korean peninsula.

5.2.1 Populations of South and North Korea

Population size and structure provide an important baseline for understanding characteristics of a society and to prepare plans for the future. The United Nations (2017) estimates that the population of North Korea was 25 million in 2015, compared to 50 million in South Korea. The total population of North Korea is currently half as big as the South Korean population (Figure 35). This also means that the relative demographic weight of the DPRK is higher than that of the GDR compared to the FRG (about 1:4) at the time of reunification. The total population of North and South Korea was 75.8 million as of 2015, ranking it twentieth largest country in the world by population.

Figure 35: Population development of the Democratic People's Republic of Korea and the Republic of Korea 1950-2015

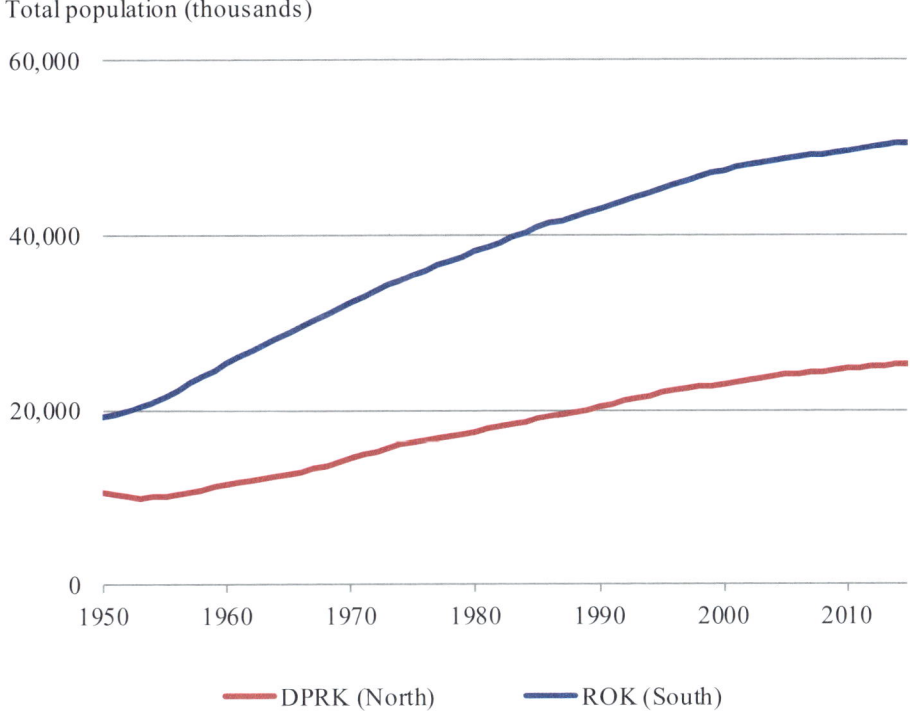

Source: United Nations 2017

The population pyramid of North Korea displays a constrictive pattern implying slow population growth and also reflects the historical events and social changes in a society (Figure 36). For instance, the Korean War (1953) caused excess mortality (particularly for males) among the birth cohorts born before 1950, the elderly population over 65 in 2015. The population of the 60- 64 age group is smaller than others, which is associated with low birth rates during the war. The 50-54 and 55-60 age groups, baby boomers born in 1955-1963, show the biggest population in the pyramid. The dip in population among the 35-39 age groups is attributable to the small size of their parent's generation (the 60-64 age groups). The population in their early twenties is smaller than the largest 45-49 age groups implying low birth rates and the excessive deaths during the famine in the 1990s.

Figure 36: Population Pyramid of Democratic People's Republic of Korea 2015

Age group

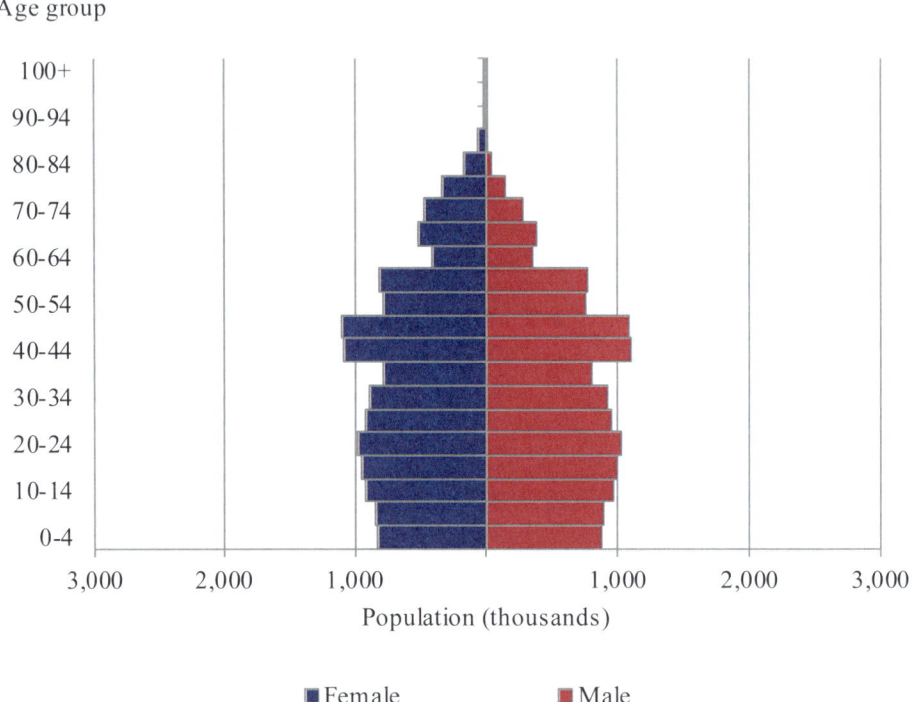

Source: United Nations 2017

In contrast, the population pyramid of South Korea has a regular pentagon shape (Figure 37). The Korean War similarly affected the population structure of South Korea, which is evidenced by the smaller size of the 60-64 age groups and older. Nonetheless, the population of South Korea in their forties and fifties is twice the size or larger than that of North Korea. By contrast, the population under 15 is just 7.0 million, reflecting sustained low fertility in recent decades.

Both pyramids have similarities in that females are more populous than males among the group aged 60 or older. The gender imbalance among the elderly is attributable to differences in mortality by gender and excessive deaths of males during the Korean War. South Korea used to show an abnormally high sex ratio at birth (SRB) in the 1980s and 1990s, partly because of sex-selective abortions caused by a preference for sons (Park and Cho 1995; Kim 2004; Yoo, Hayford, and Agadjanian 2017). The SRB has declined since the 1990s and eventually returned to normal levels in the late 2000s in South Korea whereas such an imbalanced SRB has not yet appeared in North Korea.

Figure 37: Population Pyramid of Republic of Korea 2015

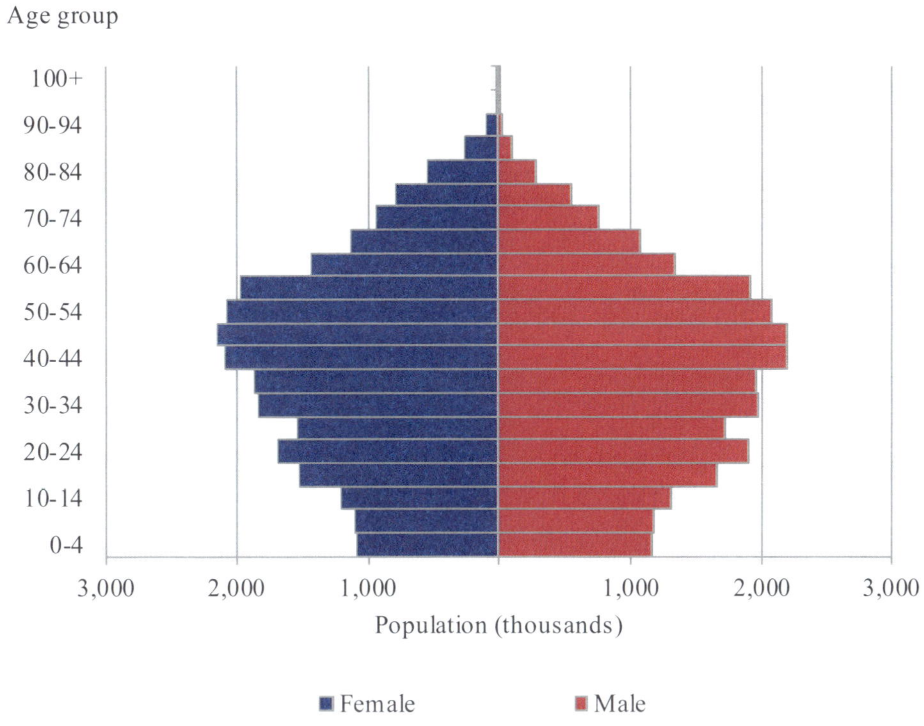

Age group

Female   Male

Source: United Nations 2017

5.2.2   Fertility and marriage

South Korea, like all post-industrial societies, has experienced a rapid decline in fertility since industrialization started in the late 1960s. The total fertility rate (TFR) of South Korea was about 6.0 or above in 1960 and reached below replacement level in 1983 (Figure 38). The TFR has further declined and remained below 1.3, "the lowest-low fertility level," since 2001. In 2016, the TFR of Korea is 1.17, which represents one of the lowest levels in the world.

Figure 38: Trends in total fertility rates of the ROK and the DPRK by 5-year period
1950-2015

Total fertility rate

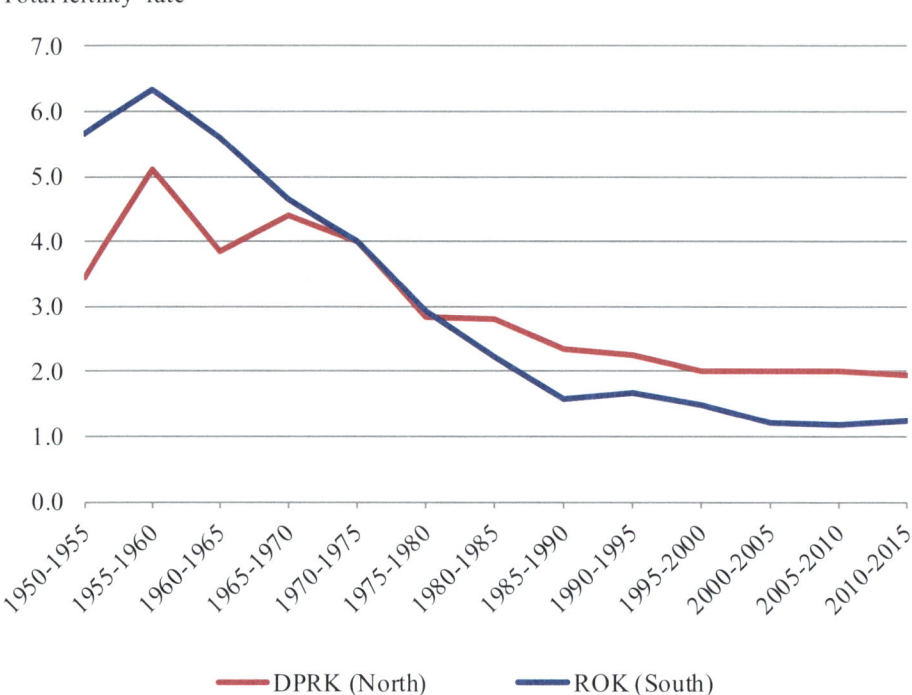

Source: United Nations 2017

The causes of low fertility are diverse. Improvements in educational attainments, an increase in female labor force participation and social activities, and change in values and
attitudes toward family and childbearing are often considered main causes of low fertility.
While institutions of gender equality have rapidly developed, traditional gender roles and
systems remain in most parts of the society. As a result, many women have difficulty
balancing work and family and often postpone or avoid marriage and childbearing. Economic restructuring and labor market change since the 1997 Asian Financial Crisis has also
contributed to increasing economic insecurity among young generations. The primary
childbearing ages have changed from their mid to late twenties to early thirties while mean
ages at first marriage and first childbearing have risen to age 30 or older for both men and
women in recent years (Figure 39). As a result, the fertility of South Korea is expected to
decline further or remain at very low levels in the near future unless a fundamental change
in marriage and childbearing occur.

Figure 39: Comparison of age-specific fertility rates between North and South Korea 2015

Age-specific fertility rate (per 1,000)

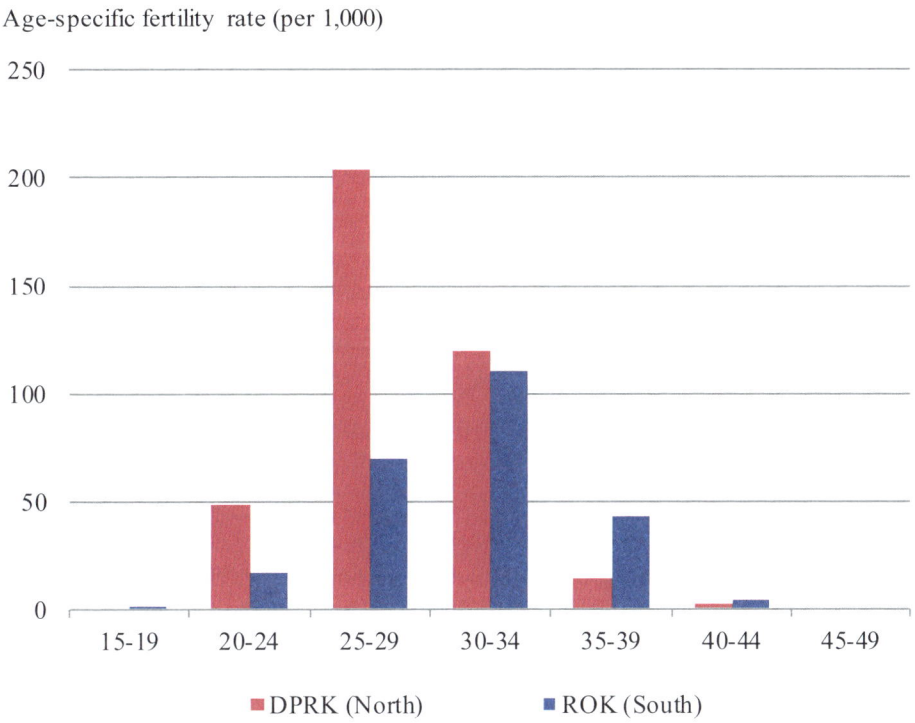

Source: United Nations 2017

According to the United Nations (2017), North Korea experienced a similar downward trend in fertility until the early 1980s. The TFR of North Korea was 5.12 in 1955-1960 but declined to 2.85 in 1975-1980, hence lower than South Korea (2.92). However, the fertility trends on both sides have separated since 1980. The TFR of North Korea has declined moderately and remains at slightly higher levels compared to the South. According to the 1993 and 2008 censuses, the TFR of North Korea is estimated to be 2.13 in 1993 and 2.00 in 2008. In the period between the two censuses, the TFR seems to have fluctuated. A few studies point out that the TFR dropped in the 1990s famine but rebounded to 2.00 in 2010, although the trend varies from 1.80 to 1.96 (e.g., Kim et al. 2011; Spoorenberg and Schwekendiek 2012). In the north, below replacement level of fertility was reached between 1993 and 1997, which is 10-15 years later than in South Korea. The TFR was 1.89 in 2014, suggesting a moderate decline in fertility after the 2008 census (DPRK Central Bureau of Statistics 2015). The drop in fertility was more pronounced among women residing in rural areas while fertility was still higher in rural areas (1.97) compared to urban areas (1.84).

When it comes to fertility patterns, both North and South Korea are rather unique compared to other countries. The lowest-low fertility rate of South Korea is well known.

However, the fertility of North Korea is also far from ordinary patterns observed in other developing countries. Firstly, age-specific fertility rates are quite uniform, concentrating in the ages 25-34. About 52 percent of newborn births were born to women aged 25-29 while about 34 percent were born to those aged 30-34 years. The 2014 SDHS suggests that among women aged 20-29, the median age at first birth was 24.9 years. In North Korea, women's labor force participation is relatively high; 91 percent of women aged 20-24 years were employed in 2014. Because of high work participation, as well as long military service, the timing of first marriage is concentrated in women's late twenties and men's early thirties in North Korea. Secondly, around 60 percent of women have two children in their lifetime, which is comparable to South Korea. Lastly, marriage remains highly universal while childlessness is still rare. Of those aged 25-29 years, 78.8 percent of women are married, while only 38.2 percent of men that age are married (DPRK Central Bureau of Statistics 2015). The numbers of people who ever married quickly increases to 89.0 percent and 97.2 percent for men and women aged 30-34. Meanwhile, childless women occupy just 0.3 percent of the 45-49 age groups in the same report.

If a reunification of Korea is realized, fertility would probably quickly react to rapidly changing circumstances. In uncertain periods, such as economic recessions and wars, people tend to postpone marriage and childbearing. The rapid decline for the Neue Länder is described at length in this study.

This initial birth shock following reunification might also happen in Korea (Stephen 2016). Uncertainty and difficulty associated with reunification make people postpone their marriage and childbearing. In the beginning stages, economic insecurity, lack of job opportunities and the desire for a better life may be more pronounced in the north, driving more people migrate to the south. Adapting to a market economy may also take a few years or a couple of decades. All of these contribute to the factors lowering fertility rates.

The problem, however, lies in difficulty estimating the extent to which fertility will decline at the time of reunification, how long it would continue, and whether fertility rates would eventually converge with that of South Korea. For the initial birth shock in a reunified Germany, the extent of the fertility decline between pre-reunification to the trough was about 0.70 in absolute terms and 46.7 percent in relative terms. If we apply these outcomes to the Korean context, the TFR would be 1.05-1.27 as an initial birth shock, which is similar or lower than that of South Korea.

Fertility trajectories following the initial birth shock can also be considered. In a pessimistic perspective, fertility rates after the birth shock may be stabilized at very low levels that are lower or similar to that of South Korea. High youth unemployment rates and uncertain economic prospects, which already prevailed in South Korea, will remain or worsen after reunification. For young adults, decisions for long-term commitment and childbearing might be avoided and postponed. If traditional familism is shared by northern people, their adaptation and assimilation to more individualized lifestyle of the south would result in a decline in fertility. The process might be accelerated depending on how many people migrate from north to south.

On the other hand, it is also possible that fertility will return to pre-reunification levels in a few years after the initial birth shock. In a positive scenario, the gradual recuperation of fertility rates following birth shock could be assumed. While universal marriage remains, the benefits of reunification will be more pronounced for the people living in the north. For instance, even minor improvements in earnings may promote family formation and childbearing. Providing effective nutrition and healthcare services can reduce unnecessary deaths of infants and children in the north. Moreover, the timing of childbearing would be earlier younger once the military is disbanded in reunified Korea.

Fertility trajectories, however, are more likely to fall between the two scenarios. Both nations are low-fertility countries, thus the "small family model" is already established in both societies and neighboring China is not a different, high fertility "role model". Further concomitants, such as the availability of housing for young couples, for example, remain fully unclear even for today's DPRK, thus exact levels of future fertility and the time until convergence and at what level remain largely unpredictable.

5.2.3   Health, mortality and life expectancy

Life expectancy is one of indicators that reflect mortality, public health and living standards of a society. From the 1960s to the middle of the 1980s, life expectancy was similar in North and South Korea. For instance, in the north life expectancy at birth was 63.5 years for males and 69.8 for females in the period of 1980-1985, or 0.4 years higher for males and 1.9 years lower for females compared to South Korea (United Nations 2007).

The parallel trends in life expectancy improvements between north and south, however, began to diverge in the late 1980s, probably because of socioeconomic progress in South Korea. The excessive deaths in the 1990s famine lowered life expectancy at birth in North Korea. For instance, life expectancy at birth declined by 2.8 years from 68.4 to 65.6 years for males and by 3.3 years from 76.0 to 72.7 years for females in 1993 and 2008 (Kim et al., 2009). Furthermore, there is a significant urban-rural divide with 70.5 years life expectancy at birth in urban and 67.6 years in rural areas (Ri and Ho 2017).

The gap between North and South Korea (76.2 years for males and 83.0 for females) has widened considerably (KOSIS 2017).

The extent to which the 1990s famine ("Arduous March" in North Korea) affected the population of North Korea varies from study to study. However, the latest studies taking account for a drop in fertility during the famine estimated the total number of excess deaths might be between 240,000 and 420,000 (Spoorenberg and Schwekendiek 2012). As the famine lasted for several years, survivors could have suffered from a wide variety of diseases and disabilities.

North Korea has regained progress in life expectancy improvement in the early 2000s, but the large gap between North and South Korea remains. The United Nations reports that estimated life expectancy at birth is 67.2 years for males and 74.1 years for females in North Korea, which is 10.7 years and 10.3 years lower than South Korea respectively. Moreover, the famine in the 1990s may have long-term impacts on the health of North Korean people. Malnutrition makes people vulnerable to respiratory and water-borne diseases and malnutrition during the first 12 months of life is extremely harmful. Chronic malnutrition and deteriorating health can also be transferred to the next generation when these children grow up and get pregnant.

The difference of more than 10 years in life expectancy reflects a severe gap in public health and living standards between the two Koreas. The public health of North Korea requires substantial support from the international community. For instance, about 70 percent of the total population is "food insecure and highly vulnerable to shortages in food production" (United Nations 2015). Among children under five, the chronic malnutrition rate is 27.9 percent while the acute malnutrition rate is 4 percent. The infant mortality rate is 23 per 1,000 live births, which is in stark contrast with 2.7 per 1,000 live births in South Korea (KOSIS, 2017).

Other mortality indicators in reproductive health are also at high levels; the maternal mortality rate is 87 per 100,000 live births while the neonatal morality rate is 16 per 1,000 live births.

The lower standard of living, insufficient food production and lack of health facilities and medicines in North Korea might be improved once peaceful reunification happens. Like reunified Germany, the most striking progress would be expected in terms of life expectancy, mortality and morbidity when the North Korean health care system – which currently is reported to be in miserable state – is refurbished and improved.

Despite these positive prospects, poor public health and lack of health infrastructure in North Korea would remain a burden. In particular, 1.8 million children, pregnant and breastfeeding women and the elderly suffer from hunger and malnutrition (United Nations 2015). Access to essential health services is limited at most levels while deterioration of the water infrastructure and constant shortages of power fundamentally constrain access to clean water. Recurring natural disasters, such as floods and drought also exacerbate these problems threatening minimum living conditions in North Korea. The report also estimates that responding to the key priorities requires about $111 million in 2015. The provision of foods and medical supplies, restoration of water supply and building health facilities may require massive government expenditures. The poor health and lack of infrastructure contribute to a rise in diseases and disability; thus it will be a challenge for Korean social security to be solved before the path to rapid convergence in this sector can be achieved.

Change in social behaviors after reunification can also bring about unexpected outcomes. Unhealthy behaviors such as smoking and alcohol consumption might increase in the north if the economic situation would worsen or if dim prospects for the future are expected in reunified Korea. For instance, social change and adoption of a western lifestyle after German renunciation brought a rapid rise in smoking prevalence among young women in East Germany (Vogt et al. 2017). To prevent such outcomes, changes in social and health behaviors should be appropriately monitored and treated within a reunified Korea.

5.2.4 Migration

If the DPRK's regime changes and people are free to move, it is very likely that immediate migration from north to south will begin. In the short term, the sheer masses of people may be a challenge, but probably of temporary nature. In a long-term perspective, brain drain may become a challenge for the north. In East Germany, the young and talented left for West Germany earlier than others. If this is the case in Korea (and this is what most estimates and scenarios are based on), the communities in the north might suffer from a lack of labor force, imbalance of sex ratio among primary childbearing ages, depopulation and population ageing (Lee et al., 2012: 121-123).

On the other hand, migration is not problematic per se. Mass migration and active interactions between North and South Korea would contribute to developing mutual understanding and social integration between two sides that have been separated for more than six decades. Intimate contacts and relations can reduce the distinct differences in values, attitudes and behaviors in the two societies. Moreover, friendships and marriages can close the emotional distance between the two populations. The exchange of human and physical resources may also give a boost to the stagnant economy in the country. South Korea has achieved an advanced economy and technology while North Korea has natural resources and workforce. The combination of the two economics may have a great synergy effect, creating more job opportunities.

The volume of north-south migration and subsequent outcomes are uncertain and unpredictable. In preparing for possible reunification, a few studies suggest the necessity of migration controls preventing mass migrants from the north. The regulation of migration flows might be useful to prevent social unrest and to prepare appropriate policies while building capacities in the north. However, it is doubtful whether such physical controls of internal migration would be possible and effective in a reunified Korea with a non-authoritarian system.

In this context, policy providing quality education and creating employment in the north is essential for minimizing migration. In reunified Germany, internal migration from rural to urban within East Germany was activated. Opportunities for higher education and employment are considered as key draws for internal migrants within East Germany. Big and small cities in local areas of North Korea can play an important role in developing the economy and distributing goods and services (Lee et al., 2014). Given the fact that quality education, means of living and health services have been insufficient and inadequate, policy measures boosting key industries and building higher education and health facilities in hub cities can contribute to keeping the population in their communities to some extent while improving their standard of living.

5.2.5   Economy, education, urbanization

Re-unification in South Korea is not only seen as a political or patriotic imperative but very often discussed under economic premises: to what extent an open border to the DPRK could stimulate pan-Korean prosperity and also if demographic ageing in the South would be lessened and postponed by reunification (the latter aspect is critically discussed by Stephen 2016).

Education and labor force participation are important to estimate the human capital of North Korea and possible labor market-related migration soon after reunification. North Korea has a free and compulsory education system that consists of preschool (one year), primary school (five years) and secondary school (six years). Because of the compulsory 12-year system, the illiteracy rate is less than one percent among the population aged over 10 years in North Korea.

Although the literacy rate in North Korea is near 100 percent among the population aged over 10 years, the quality of secondary and tertiary education remains obscure. For instance, the curriculum is often filled with ideological training. This is true for schools and universities (Eberstadt & Banister 1992b: 524). The distribution of educational attainment among working ages is also in contrast with South Korea. Among the age group of 30-59, nearly 100 percent have completed senior secondary-school education, while those with tertiary education and above are 13.9 percent (15.8 percent for male and 11.9 percent for female). In the south, however, people who achieved tertiary education or above are 40.3 percent (46.0 percent for male and 34.4 percent for female) for the same ages, which is much higher than in North Korea.

In North Korea, most people start participating in the labor force upon completion of secondary school. The percent of the population 16 years or older working in the last week was 69.3 percent in 2014. The 2008 census used a different definition of economic activity (working in the last six months), but the percent of the working population remains similar at 70.2 percent. The retired population also was 18.6 percent, probably because the retirement age was set as 60 years for males and 55 years for females. The rural-urban difference in working people was marginal, though somewhat higher in rural (71.2 percent) than in urban (68.2 percent) areas.

One interesting aspect is the pattern of female labor force participation. Of the population 16 years or older, female labor force participation (61.6 percent) is lower than that of males (78.3 percent) in North Korea. In the 20-24 age groups, however, female labor force participation is high: as much as 91 percent. The high rate of above 80 percent continues until ages 50-54. The stable variation over primary working ages also appear in males: the male labor force participation rate is more than 95 percent in the age groups between 30 and 59, probably because of guaranteed employment. Females seem to start working early and retire early, about five years sooner compared to males, because of gender differences in educational attainment, military service and retirement ages.

The pattern of labor force participation in North Korea differs from that in South Korea. The 2015 census of South Korea suggests that the labor force participation rate (in the last week) among the population 15 years or older is 56.1 percent; 67.5 percent for males and 45.3 percent for females. As the south has a much larger old population, it is difficult to compare that directly with the north. Nevertheless, the female labor force participation rate is definitely lower in South than in North Korea. In addition, female labor force participation tends to decline during ages 30-39 for marriage and childrearing and rebound after those ages in South Korea, which is associated with traditional gender roles, work-family imbalance and the lack of childcare facilities. This is known as "M-shape" female labor force participation. In North Korea, the higher rates of female labor force participation in their twenties and thirties implies that daycare facilities are widely available. Research based on interviews with North Korean defectors reports that daycare centers are freely available for children from 1 month to 3 months, but their use is the parents' decision (Lee at al., 2011).

In the DPRK, of the working population 16 years older, 41.8 percent of people work in the primary sector (agriculture and related activities), 26.9 percent work in the secondary (manufacturing) and 31.3 percent in the tertiary (service) sector. The distribution of working sectors is also distinct by residence. Four in five persons in rural residents are engaged in the primary sector whereas only 17.3 percent of urban residents are in the same sector. Instead, urban residents are more distributed in secondary (39.6 percent) and tertiary (43.1 percent) sectors.

North Korea is also less urbanized than South Korea. In 2008, four out of ten people in the northern population resided in urban areas compared to nine out of ten of the people in the south. In the north, the proportion of urban residents has remained stable since the mid-1980s (59.0 percent in 1985) whereas urbanization is still ongoing. In the south, the pace of urbanization seems to have stagnated in recent decades. The population growth rate is low and insignificant between urban and rural areas; annual population growth rates were estimated at 0.88 percent for urban areas and 0.84 percent for rural areas in 2008 (Kim et al. 2011:167). Internal migration is limited in North Korea. Using the 2008 census of North Korea and the 2005 census of South Korea, Kim and colleagues compared internal migration patterns between the two (Kim et al. 2011). They reported that the internal migration rate for the last five years was 3.5 percent in North Korea and 33.1 percent in South Korea. This wide gap in internal migration reflects differences in economic situations and freedom to move in North and South Korea.

5.2.6   Korea as one – A challenging vision

Given the long, conflicting political situation and the decades-long hermetic separation, it is very probable that huge efforts will be needed to close the cultural and emotional distance between the Republic of Korea and the DPRK. The separation cannot be compared with the German case where, although a death zone secured the inner German border, Willy Brandt's Ostpolitik fell on fertile soil and some low profile but regular exchange was established. Family ties remained intact for those who wanted, political dialogue took place and there were even economic relations between the two nations. Besides the failed attempt at the so-called sunshine policy of rapprochement, mutual understanding and reconciliation in the 1990s including South Korea-financed and backed Special Economic Zones (now frozen) in the DPRK borderland (Köppen 2010), the Republic of Korea and the DPRK have basically experienced six decades of military deterrence, provocations and diplomatic stagnation. There are currently only very few friendly ties between South and North Korea.

Hence, there is a risk that prolonged alienation, disregard and prejudice towards one another may lead to a persistent gap between the two sides even if reunification is in sight. Therefore, all feasible efforts for academic and cultural exchange (e.g., research, concerts, and sports) should be continued despite intermittent provocations and concomitant international sanctions to the North. Also the idea – already included in the sunshine policy – to grant financial and technical support for research and economic development to the DPRK in order to gradually raise its wealth and prosperity from its own efforts should be considered a strategy. The stronger the northern economy is at the moment of gradual Korean integration or sudden reunification, the more feasible this undertaking will be.

One example of good practice in this vein was the financial support for conducting the 2008 census in the DPRK, which was provided by the government of South Korea.

Food security and poor public health are urgent problems in North Korea today, which may have long-term impacts on demography, society and economics It is estimated that more than two-thirds of the population of North Korea suffer from food insecurity. Chronic malnutrition and ineffective medical treatment make people vulnerable in various dimensions. Poor health resulting from malnutrition and its consequences is a severe problem for North Korea's perspectives in the future. The government of a reunified Korea should definitively prioritize health infrastructure needs and investment. At the beginning of Korean integration, international help from the humanitarian community would very probably also be needed.

In South Korea, as a typical low fertility society, demographic change with a rapidly ageing society became a central concern of social policy and cohesion, as increasing expenses for social security are expected. The hypothetical integration of an unknown number of needy North Korean people (either due to poor labor market qualifications or because of health problems) in the case of reunification is considered a potentially unmanageable risk. Given the decreasing birth rates of the DPRK, the rejuvenation of a reunified Korea (and postponement of demographic change) will only last a short time. Aside from these demography-related, critical imponderables, rebuilding and improving North Korea's economic and public infrastructure would remain an even more costly and enormous challenge. Economic and social instability as a consequence of Korean reunification is a concern for policy makers.

Naming reunification-related unknowns and burdens is crucial for developing suitable strategies. A failed reunification cannot be the aim, but instead Korean integration to end the long-lasting enmity and military tensions between North and South. The latter is a major factor that is ruining the DPRK's economic potential by investing manpower (and womanpower) as well as knowledge and scarce financial resources in the military complex.

As much as German reunification was an unprecedented venture, the possible integration of both Korean states in one entity and society would involve far more imponderables than certitudes. A fail-proof scenario for strategic planning is impossible. However, an integrated approach through interdisciplinary discussion does offer ideas for possible settings and different options.

Demographic development is one important basis in this respect, but not the only key to success. The main issue remains the ability to financially facilitate reunification or integration for Korea.

6 Concluding thoughts on a Germany-inspired Korea scenario

The two states on the Korean peninsula have been divided for more than six decades; most of that era has been characterized by severe militarized political tensions and only a short period of rapprochement. Nevertheless, peaceful coexistence, stability, openness for reconciliation and the vision of a possible reunification remain pivotal paradigms for the Republic of Korea's politics. Prosperity is intrinsically tied to peace and stability. In this context – and despite repeated setbacks in realpolitik – research on Korean reunification scenarios as a union of equals or in the form of gradual integration represents not only a field of theoretical academic research, but also a field of applied policy advice.

For Korean scenarios, German reunification is perceived as prototypical reference, although the preconditions – geopolitical, socio-economic and cultural settings – are very different[1]. However, if the German case is not perceived as some kind of model, but rough scheme and outline, it can provide useful knowledge for scenario building. Especially in the field of population studies, the above-described idea of "careful forecasting" can provide reliable results. This is because not all mutations and changes in demography are solely linked to cultural, political and socio-economic settings and their interdependencies, but often bound to universal patterns that are inherent to human behavior and more or less predictable.

After careful consideration, four main axes of demographic and societal trends linked to reunification or gradual integration on the Korean peninsula appear likely without much of a doubt.

6.1 Social freezing and low fertility

With a radical system change in North Korea in the course of Korean integration, an immediate period of uncertainty and "social freezing" is to be expected. Therefore a similar decline in fertility, as it was the case in the Neue Länder, will probably characterize the first years after the event of system change, with a gradual increase afterwards. Like Germany, it is unlikely that North Korean fertility would rebound to the pre-unification TFR/CFR level, but a similar level of fertility all over Korea will hold. This assumption is based on two considerations: Firstly, the DPRK's fertility has been gradually declining for decades. Hence, low fertility is already a trend without reunification and an eventual adoption of "imported" low-fertility leitbilder, etc. This North Korean decline has also gone on for too long (and is too stable) to be explained as a temporary aftermath of the famine between 1994 and 1998. Thus, with a TFR of around 2.0 according to the 2008 census, the DPRK is already on its way to below replacement fertility or has already passed the tipping point. Secondly, after reunification or in the course of Korean integration, new lifestyle forms (individualism) and new leitbilder will change North Koreans' behavior. Since North Korea is "framed" by two (extreme) low fertility countries, China and South Korea, which will probably serve as "role models" (already today, fashion and lifestyle elements from China

---

[1]   Having said that, we must acknowledge that there also is no other example of reunification or a reunification-like occurrence in history that is more similar than the Korean and the German case in a broader historical, geopolitical setting and the form of national division.

and South Korea partially infiltrate the DPRK's society, e.g., via – illegally – imported DVDs of films, soap operas, etc.), their family and fertility model will also prevail. The idea of a possible "enthusiastic" post-unification baby boom instead is rather unlikely. The currently higher fertility of North Korean women will not become the norm or model for the South. Hence, reunified Korea would very probably be a below replacement fertility level society and speculations on long-term rejuvenation of Korean society due to reunification (as it is sometimes hoped for in South Korean discourses on national unification) should be rejected.

6.2   Leaps in health and life expectancy

Compared to the high level in South Korea, healthcare (mainly infrastructure and provision of pharmaceuticals) and the lasting negative heritage of the 1990s famine represent extremely weak factors in the DPRK. Consequently, there are also significant gaps in life expectancy at birth, morbidity and mortality.

The example of Germany proved that with improvements to the healthcare infrastructure and the provision of the latest methods of treatment, a rapid increase in life expectancy at all levels and an immediate decline in mortality, especially premature deaths by curable diseases or accidents, takes place. This positive development in Germany was, however, based on an existing and well-organized GDR healthcare system of generally good quality. Hence, the improvements in healthcare quality were immediately and easily accessible to the citizens in the Neue Länder.

For the DPRK, however, the real state of infrastructure, capabilities and capacities of healthcare staff and medical doctors, etc. are unknown and the little information available offers a rather alarming picture. According to the international Healthcare Access and Quality Index, the Republic of Koreas is assessed with an "A" rating (High performance in global perspective), while the DPRK is classified on "C" level (Medium performance in global perspective) (GBD 2015 Healthcare Access and Quality Collaborators 2017). Therefore, upon integration/reunification, immediate and massive investments in North Korea's public healthcare should be given highest priority. In this phase of refurbishment and investment, no striking positive leaps and bounds but mainly gradual improvements in terms of health, life expectancy and mortality should be expected; mainly through simple factors, such as the distribution/availability of pharmaceuticals that were previously unavailable. After this time lag though, a rapid change for the better – as in Germany – is very likely. The direct and indirect long-lasting impact of the "Arduous March" famine on the average state of health, mortality and life expectancy in reunified Korea is very difficult to estimate. In a long-term perspective, however, convergence with South Korea will likely occur within two to three decades.

6.3   The challenge of migration

Given the accentuated wealth gap between the DPRK and all neighboring countries of South Korea, China and the Russian Federation, a regime change and the possibility of free movement within the country and outside the state will very probably encourage massive migration. Especially north-south migration flux should be expected. Like the German example, where the collapse of the GDR regime and reunification were intrinsically linked to emigration, a similar scenario can be expected for Korea. To recap the broader picture in Germany: Alongside mass demonstrations against the government, a wave of emigration to West Germany via the Hungarian-Austrian border (an estimated 25,000 people between spring of 1989 and the fall of the Iron Curtain) and via the courtyard of the Federal Republic of Germany's embassy in Prague[2] (Czechoslovakia) took place. The massive east-west immigration after the border was officially opened soon led to fears of destabilization in both countries, the GDR and the FRG. As a consequence, to slowdown this exodus, the economic and monetary union was drafted, agreed upon and implemented within a remarkably short time. Thus, migration (including cross-border commuting over a longer perspective) is likely to also become a key challenge in the course of Korean integration, also because the relative proportion of North Koreans to South Koreans at 1:2 is much larger than the German ratio of about 1:4.

However, this expected massive migration would be physically channeled to much fewer existing border-crossing points than in Germany (there were 10 in Berlin and 11 between the national GDR/FRG border not including railway border crossings in 1989). In Korea, only three potential border crossings (Kaesong, Panmunjon, Gaesong) are available. Considering the military securing of the Demilitarized Zone including anti-personnel mines as well as large strips of restricted areas close to the DMZ, along with the former battlefield of the Korean War and remaining mines and unexploded ordinance devices, there are not many options for crossing the border elsewhere so rapid construction of improvised border crossings will be necessary.

The North Korean-Chinese and North Korean-Russian borders are much less secured. Illegally wading through Tumen River, marking most of this border, is possible at many places. People fleeing North Korea to China choose this option and also illegal patty trading between China and the DPRK has been reported. Thus, illegal migration and commercial networks between China and North Korea do exist. The short Russian-Korean border plays practically no role, as the border is rather short at 17 km, easy to control and no major settlement is located nearby (the town-like Russian settlement of Chassan serves as a railway border crossing but has less than 1,000 inhabitants).

The above-mentioned ties and contacts with China may have an impact on the direction and volume of North Korean emigration after a regime change. Furthermore, the Chinese border province to Korea is inhabited by about 2 million Chinese citizens of Korean ethnicity. Hence, leaving the DPRK towards China might become an interesting option instead of heading for South Korea, especially if the Republic of Korea's government should decide to hinder mass immigration to the South. It is even possible that a significant migration may head towards China from the beginning, given the existing ties and potentially easier access to the Chinese border zone. So, unlike the German situation, where the FRG (later Alte Länder) were the major and basically only alternative as country/region of destination, China might become important in terms of emigration in the case of Korea.

By all means, significant migration pressure from the DPRK towards its neighbors in the north and south should be anticipated in the case of a regime change though the political

---

[2]   Until September 30, 1989, about 4,000 GDR refugees fled into the West German embassy. Starting October 1, the emigration of these people in trains from Prague via GDR territory to the FRG began. This was made possible after negotiations between the FRG and GDR. On October 3 – despite the departure of the first wave of embassy refugees – more than 5,000 GDR refugees made it into the embassy, another 2,000 asked for asylum on the public square in front of the embassy building.

reaction to this by the People's Republic of China and the Republic of Korea in particular remains unpredictable. A full opening of South Korea to North Korean immigrants would very probably channel migration to the South. A strict border regime at the DMZ with very restricted access would probably encourage (illegal) emigration to China and maybe the Russian Federation (and further beyond via China/Russia). Additionally, rural-urban migration towards the major cities of Pyongyang, Hamhung, Namp'o, Hungnam and Kaesong (the latter as a potential steppingstone to South Korea, given its proximity to the border and existing border crossing) can be expected. Currently, internal migration in the DPRK is restricted by the regime; thus an increase in internal migration is very likely under all variants of change towards a non-authoritarian regime. Therefore, besides rural-urban internal migration, other patterns of internal migration will also emerge: from peripheral areas to more promising regions in terms of standard of living and employment. Thus, rural-urban disparities are likely to increase.

The current DMZ and CCZ (the 7 to 30 km-wide Civilian Control Zone on the South Korean side of the DMZ) represent peripheral regions with low dynamics. This could potentially change after an opening of the border, because daily or weekly cross-border commuting of North Koreans to South Korea for work may become an important phenomenon. However, for this scenario infrastructure and respective job opportunities (perhaps through concerted investments in the – then – former border region) would be essential. For the Seoul agglomeration, massive flows of cross-border commuters can be expected as soon as the border is open. This assumption is based on the relative proximity of Seoul/Sugdowon Metropolitan Region to the 300,000 inhabitants of Kaesong city in the Hwanghae-pukto region (about 1.7 million inhabitants) in North Korea (Kaesong is about a 60 km drive from Seoul) and the fact that an efficient street and railway border crossing was built for the former joint Korean Kaesong Special Economic Zone/Kaesong Industrial Zone (established in 2002 and operational from 2005 until 2016). Furthermore, in the Kaesong Special Economic Zone, an estimated 53,000 North Korean workers have been working in South Korean factories (Köppen 2010). Thus, it is without much doubt that these people and their close friends and relatives in particular will be prone to take a chance finding work in nearby Sugdowon Metropolitan Region.

Random, uncoordinated mass migration to South Korea and the destabilization of both states in the case of a political collapse of the DPRK is a fear in the Republic of Korea. Thus, an initially strict border regime paralleled by humanitarian aid in North Korea and monetary policy to prevent massive migration is a likely option for scenario building.

6.4   Social transformation and challenge

Very little is known about the cultural proximity or distance between the North and South Korean people after 60 years of radical separation. Thus, it is hard to estimate to what extent alienation, misleading images and expectations concerning the respective other may hamper Korean integration once it is in reach. The fact that the language has started to develop in different ways to an extent that this become a concern of South and North Korean linguists (The Guardian, 07/11/2014) and complaints by North Korean defectors in the Republic of Korea about being discriminated against (Daily North Korea, 03/17/2017, McCelvey 2016) suggest a serious potential for socio-cultural friction in the case of reunification. Although both Korean states show a high degree of ethnic homogeneity with very low numbers of foreigners (unknown for the DPRK; between 2 percent and 3 percent in

South Korea), efforts in inner-Korean intercultural training and sensibility concerning mutual respect are advisable. This is especially important as the presupposed socio-cultural gap will very probably be extended by further social and economic separating factors in a long-term perspective.

Very probably, a high percentage of the North Korean workforce is not sufficiently trained for the demands of a post-modern, globalized economy as established in the south. Thus during an initial phase, North Korea will remain underperforming compared to the south and the closure of non-competitive businesses, a prevalence of low wage jobs and rocketing and long-lasting high unemployment rates in all sectors must be expected. This situation may increase migration out of the north and create the emergence of an extensive North Korean underclass. Disappointment and exasperation would be likely consequences. Therefore, immediate investments in education, re-training and on-the-job training as well as efficient economic subsidies and a social security system would be important pillars to make reunification a success. The implementation of training and education "hot spots" (e.g., with training centers, universities, technical colleges and vocational schools) in North Korea might be a feasible strategy to ease catch-up modernization and prevent migration to the south, mainly of the young generation.

Despite such efforts, this first stage of reunification will probably produce a lost generation of those who are unable to adapt to the new socio-cultural and economic conditions for various reasons (e.g., lack of skills, discrimination, age). This is why the above-mentioned issue of social security and social cohesion needs to be addressed. Quality of life and satisfaction are key elements in a truly reunified nation. Thus, these elements should not be neglected, especially as Germany shows that almost three decades after reunification, despite huge efforts and objective success, full convergence still remains unachieved.

6.5   German reunification – No blueprint for Korea but a valuable knowledge base

Given the quite unique character and circumstances of German reunification, it is not really possible for studies of the German case to lead to fail-proof blueprints for Korean scenarios. However, such an undertaking delivers valuable knowledge on demographic patterns after a union of societies. Scenarios on Korean reunification and projections based on the German pathway in terms of demography, cultural and socio-economic trends lack particularly comprehensive, reliable information about the population, society, cultural specifics, state of economy and infrastructure. Safe projections on demographic and socio-economic changes after Korean unity would need at least basic knowledge of various additional issues: institutions, cultural norms, leitbild, typical hopes and dreams, for example.

Too little is "really" known about the DPRK. Thus, an indispensable basis for scenarios and strategy is missing. This also means that more in-depth guesses on the tangible demographic consequences of Korean reunification or integration than the assumptions presented above on fertility, health/mortality and migration would be extremely uncertain. As a consequence, detailed long-term scenarios do not make sense. Based on the German experience, however, a rough path may be described. Korean reunification would probably lead to a more or less prolonged phase of social freezing in North Korea, followed by a phase of accelerated convergence in socio-economic terms. Having reached a tipping point, this approximation will slow down and a north-south gap concerning various aspects will remain. These gaps may gradually change and reflect not merely Korean division but regional disparities. Furthermore, specific behavior and patterns (maybe even institutions) of DPRK "style" or heritage will persist (and even prevail in some fields). After almost 30 years after reunification, the German experience shows that catch-up modernization can be expected for the initial phase of Korean integration. However, hybridization – with probably more elements of convergence than divergence – is the most likely demographic, socio-cultural and socio-economic pathway of development. A rapid leveling of living conditions and economic efficiency should not be expected. North-south disparities in a long-term perspective will be characteristic for reunified Korea.

In any case, regardless of whether Korean fast-track reunification or gradual integration of the DPRK and the Republic of Korea is the focus, very extensive financial efforts are inevitable. In the light of the current huge gaps between the DPRK and South Korea in terms of economic performance and prosperity, social cohesion after reunification will represent a surging challenge of highest priority. Thus, significant, long-lasting south-north transfers plus immediate tangible action to establish the basis for prosperity and to guarantee cohesion must be realized. Along with this aspect, a crucial obstacle and blind-spot needs to be addressed: it is unknown whether South Korea's economy and financial potential are so performant and well-resourced that a reunification under today's preconditions with regard to the huge gap between the DPRK and the Republic of Korea in virtually all relevant sectors is feasible at all. Thus, the above-mentioned strategy of step-by-step integration seems to be the preferable, if not the only, alternative for reunification.

That said, allow us to bring to mind once again that our study on demographic aspects of German reunification and possible knowledge for a hypothetical integration of the DPRK and the Republic of Korea is neither a fully comprehensive tract on the German example nor a strategic recommendation for Korea. It is, rather, a partly explorative contribution to the field of comparative reunification research and should serve to encourage further systematic scholarly demographic research on the consequences and heritage of German reunification in a long-term perspective.

References

Ahbe, Thomas; Hofmann, Michael (2002): Eigentlich unsere beste Zeit. Erinnerungen an den DDR Alltag in unterschiedlichen Milieus. In: Aus Politik und Zeitgeschichte, B 17/2002: 13-22.

Beck, Ulrich (1992): Risk Society: Towards a New Modernity. London: Sage Publications.

Beck, Ulrich; Beck-Gernsheim, Elisabeth (1993): Nicht Autonomie, sondern Bastelbiographie: Anmerkungen zur Individualisierungsdiskussion am Beispiel des Aufsatzes von Günter Burkart. Zeitschrift für Soziologie 22,3: 178–87.

Behrendt, Holger (2010): Regionale Analyse der Mortalität in den alten und neuen Bundesländern. Lohmar, Köln: Eul Verlag.

Berlin-Institut für Bevölkerung und Entwicklung (Ed.) (2016): Im Osten auf Wanderschaft. Wie Umzüge die demografische Landkarte zwischen Rügen und Erzgebirge verändern. Berlin.

Bernardi, Laura; Keim, Sylvia; Von der Lippe, Holger (2007): Social Influences on Fertility. A Comparative Mixed Methods Study in Eastern and Western Germany. In: Journal of Mixed Methods Research 1,1: 23-47.

Boehnke, Mandy (2013): Hochschulbildung und Kinderlosigkeit. Deutsch-deutsche Unterschiede. In: Konietzka, Dirk; Kreyenfeld, Michaela (Eds.): Ein Leben ohne Kinder. Ausmaß, Strukturen und Ursachen von Kinderlosigkeit. Wiesbaden: Springer VS: 81-100.

Borowicc, Steven (2014): Two Koreas make strides to talk the same language. The Guardian. 11.07.2014. https://www.theguardian.com/world/2014/jul/11/korean-peoples-comprehensive-dictionary (last accessed 15.09.2017).

Bucher, Hansjörg (2002): Die Sterblichkeit in den Regionen der Bundesrepublik Deutschland und deren Ost-West-Lücke seit der Einigung. In: Cromm, Jürgen; Scholz, Rembrandt D. (Eds.): Regionale Sterblichkeit in Deutschland. Göttingen: WiSoMed Verlag: 33-38.

Bujard, Martin (2015): Kinderlosigkeit in Deutschland: Wie interagieren Bildung, Wohnort, Migrationshintergrund, Erwerbstätigkeit und Kohorte? In: Zeitschrift für Familienforschung 27 (3): 255-269.

Bujard, Martin; Dorbritz, Jürgen (Eds.) (2015): Kinderlosigkeit und Kinderreichtum in Deutschland. Analysen mit Daten des Mikrozensus 2012. In: Zeitschrift für Familienforschung 3: Leverkusen

Bujard, Martin; Sulak, Harun (2016): Mehr Kinderlose oder weniger Kinderreiche? In: Kölner Zeitschrift für Soziologie und Sozialpsychologie 68 (3): 487-514.

Bundesamt für Bauwesen und Raumordnung – BBR –, Bundesinstitut für Bau-, Stadt- und Raumforschung – BBSR – (Eds.) (2012): Raumordnungsbericht 2011. Bonn.

Bundesministerium für Wirtschaft und Energie (BMWi) (2017): Jahresbericht der Bundesregierung zum Stand der Deutschen Einheit. Berlin.

Bundeszentrale für politische Bildung (2015): Die Frage nach den Kosten der Wiedervereinigung. Online 28.09.2015 http://www.bpb.de/geschichte/deutsche-einheit/zahlen-und-fakten-zur-deutschen-einheit/212659/die-frage-nach-den-kosten-der-wiedervereinigung last retrieved 07.09.2017.

Cassens, Insa; Luy, Marc; Scholz, Rembrandt (Eds.) (2009): Die Bevölkerung in Ost- und Westdeutschland – Demografische, gesellschaftliche und wirtschaftliche Entwicklungen seit der Wende. Wiesbaden: Springer VS.

Conrad, Christoph; Lechner, Michael; Werner, Welf (1996): "East German fertility after unification: Crisis or adaptation?" Population and Development Review 22(2): 331–358.

Diabaté, Sabine (2015): Mutter Leitbilder: Spagat zwischen Autonomie und Aufopferung. In: Schneider, Norbert F.; Diabaté, Sabine; Ruckdeschel, Kerstin (Eds.): FamilienLeitbilder in Deutschland. Kulturelle Vorstellungen zu Partnerschaft, Elternschaft und Familienleben. Beiträge zur Bevölkerungswissenschaft 48. Opladen: Barbara Budrich: 207-26.

Diabaté, Sabine (2015): Mutterleitbilder: Spagat zwischen Autonomie und Aufopferung. In: Schneider et al. (Eds.): Familienleitbilder in Deutschland. Kulturelle Vorstellung zu Partnerschaft, Elternschaft und Familienleben. Opladen: Budrich.

Diabaté, Sabine; Lück, Detlev (2014): Familienleitbilder – Identifikation und Wirkungsweise auf generatives Verhalten. Zeitschrift für Familienforschung 26,1: 49–69.

Diabaté, Sabine; Lück, Detlev; Schneider, Norbert F. (2015): Leitbilder der Elternschaft: Zwischen Kindeswohl und fairer Aufgabenteilung. In: Schneider, Norbert F.; Diabaté, Sabine; Ruckdeschel, Kerstin (Eds.): Familienleitbilder in Deutschland. Kulturelle Vorstellungen zu Partnerschaft, Elternschaft und Familienleben. Beiträge zur Bevölkerungswissenschaft 48. Opladen: Barbara Budrich: 247-67.

Dinkel, Reiner H. (2003): Die Sterblichkeitsunterschiede zwischen dem östlichen und westlichen Teil Deutschlands seit der Wende. Die Lehren aus einigen überraschenden Entwicklungen. In: Sitzungsberichte der Leibniz-Sozietät 62,6: 65-87.

Dorbritz, Jürgen (2008): Germany: Family diversity with low actual and desired fertility. In: Demographic Research 19: 557–598.

Eberstadt, Nicholas; Banister, Judith (1992a): The Population of North Korea. Institute of East Asian Studies. Berkeley: University of California.

Eberstadt, Nicholas; Banister, Judith (1992b): "Divided Korea: Demographic and Socioeconomic Issues for Reunification." In: Population and Development Review 18(3): 505-531.

Eckart, Karl (1989): DDR - Geographische Strukturen, Daten, Entwicklungen. Stuttgart.

Fink, Sebastian; Jacobs, Olaf (2014): So leben wir. Eine Bestandsaufnahme in Ostdeutschland. In: Schriftenreihe der Bundeszentrale für politische Bildung. Bd. 1491: Bonn.

Freitag, K.; Spiegel, R.; Wendt, Hartmut (1989): Computer Atlas Demographie Bevölkerungsentwicklung und territoriale Bevölkerungsstruktur in der ehemaligen DDR. Akademie der Wissenschaften, Berlin: Bauinformation (76): Berlin.

Friedrich, Klaus (2008): 16 Jahre innerdeutsche Ost–West–Migration. Eine Einführung in die Transformation eines geschlossenen Migrationsregimes in die Postmoderne. In: Friedrich, Klaus; Schultz, Andrea (Eds.): Brain drain oder brain circulation? Konsequenzen und Perspektiven der Ost-West-Migration. In: forum ifl 8: 13-20.

Friedrich, Klaus; Schultz, Andrea (2005): Mit einem Bein noch im Osten? Abwanderung aus Ostdeutschland in sozialgeographischer Perspektive. In: Dienel, Christiane (Ed.): Abwanderung, Geburtenrückgang und regionale Entwicklung. Ursachen und Folgen des Bevölkerungsrückgangs in Ostdeutschland. Wiesbaden: 203-216.

Fuwa, Makiko (2004): Macro–level Gender Inequality and the Division of Household Labor in 22 Countries. In: American Sociological Review 69: 751–67.

Gabriel, Oscar W.; Holtmann, Everhard; Jaeck, Tobias; Leidecker-Sandmann, Melanie; Maier, Jürgen; Maier, Michaela (2015): Deutschland 25. Gesellschaftliche Trends und politische Einstellungen. (=Zeitbilder, Bundeszentrale für Politische Bildung). Bonn

Gärtner, Karla; Mühlichen, Michael (2012): Die Entwicklung der Verkehrsunfallsterblichkeit. In: Bevölkerungsforschung Aktuell 33,1: 6-9.

GBD (2015): Healthcare Access and Quality Collaborators (2017): Healthcare Access and Quality Index based on mortality from causes amenable to personal health care in 195 countries and territories, 1990-2015: a novel analysis from the Global Burden of Disease Study 2015 (2017). In: Lancet 390 (10091): 231–266.

Geißler, Rainer (2002): Nachholende Modernisierung mit Widersprüchen. In: Aus Politik und Zeitgeschichte, Bundeszentrale für politische Bildung. http://www.bpb.de/apuz/25413/nachholende-modernisierung-mit-widerspruechen?p=all

Geißler, Rainer (2014): Die Sozialstruktur Deutschlands. Zur gesellschaftlichen Entwicklung mit einer Bilanz der Vereinigung. 7. Aufl. Wiesbaden.

Gjonça, Arjan; Brockmann, Hilke; Maier, Heiner (2000): "Old-age mortality in Germany prior to and after Reunification". Demographic Research 3(1).

Gjonça, Arjan; Brockmann, Hilke; Maier, Heiner (2000): Old-Age Mortality in Germany prior to and after Reunification. In: Demographic Research 3,1.

Goldstein, Joshua R.; Kreyenfeld, Micheala (2011): "Has East Germany Overtaken West Germany? Recent Trends in Order-Specific Fertility". In: Population and Development Review 37(3): 453-72.

Grünheid, Evelyn (2015): Regionale Aspekte des demografischen Wandels. Wiesbaden.

Grünheid, Evelyn; Sulak, Harun (2016): Bevölkerungsentwicklung 2016. Daten, Fakten, Trends zum demografischen Wandel. Wiesbaden.

Hakim, Catherine (2003): Models of the Family in Modern Societies: In: Ideals and Realities. Ashgate.

Heske, Gerhard (2009): Volkswirtschaftliche Gesamtrechnung DDR 1950–1989. Daten, Methoden, Vergleiche (HSR-Supplement No. 21). Köln.

Heiland, Frank (2004): Trends in East-West German Migration from 1989 to 2002. In: Demographic Research 11,7: 173-194.

Huinink, Johannes; Kreyenfeld, Michaela; Trappe, Heike (Eds.) (2012): Familie und Partnerschaft in Ost- und Westdeutschland. Ähnlich und doch immer noch anders. In: Zeitschrift für Familienforschung 9.

Kibele, Eva U. B. (2012): Regional Mortality Differences in Germany. Demographic Research Monographs 10. Dordrecht et al.: Springer.

Kibele, Eva U. B.; Scholz, Rembrandt D. (2009): Trend der Mortalitätsdifferenzen in Ost und West unter Berücksichtigung der vermeidbaren Sterblichkeit. In: Cassens, Insa; Luy, Marc; Scholz, Rembrandt D. (Eds.): Die Bevölkerung in Ost- und Westdeutschland: Demografische, gesellschaftliche und wirtschaftliche Entwicklungen seit der Wende. Wiesbaden: VS Verlag für Sozialwissenschaften: 124-139.

Kim, Doo-Sub (2004): "Missing Girls in South Korea: Trends, Levels, and Regional Variations." In: Population 59(6): 865-878.

Kim, Doo-Sub; Choe, Minja K.; Jun, K.H.; Lee, Seungil; Kim, H. S. (2011): The Population of North Korea and Population Census. In: Statistics Korea. Daejoen: Statistics Korea.

Klein, Olaf Georg (2002): Warum Ost- und Westdeutsche aneinander vorbeireden. In: Aus Politik und Zeitgeschichte, B 37-38/2002: 3-5.

Klüsener, Sebastian; Goldstein, Joshua R. (2016): A Long-Standing Demographic East-West Divide in Germany. In: Population Space and Place (published online 22 July 2014 in Wiley Online Library). [doi: 10.1002/psp.1870].

KOSIS (2017): Korean Statistical Information Service. Kosis.kr.

Köppen, Bernhard (2005): Stadtentwicklung zwischen Schrumpfung und Sprawl. Auswirkungen der Stadt-Umland-Wanderungen im Verdichtungsraum Chemnitz-Zwickau. In: Tönning et al. Der Andere Verlag.

Köppen, Bernhard (2010): Special Economic Zones (SEZs) Along the Korean Demilitarised Zone. A Feasible Pathway Towards An Accessible North Korea? In: Quaestiones Geographicae 29 (4): 95-109.

Kown, Bae Min (2017): Report reveals continuing discrimination of defectors in South Korea. Daily North Korea 17.03.2017. http://www.dailynk.com/english/read.php?cataId=nk00100&num=14423.

Kühntopf, Stephan; Stedtfeld, Susanne (2012): Wenige junge Frauen im ländlichen Raum: Ursachen und Folgen der selektiven Abwanderung in Ostdeutschland. BiB Working Paper 3: Wiesbaden.

Kuppe, Johannes L. (2001): Vom Charme neuer deutscher Gelassenheit. Die Vereinigung Deutschlands – Glücksfall oder Danaergeschenk der Geschichte? In: Aus Politik und Zeitgeschichte, B 39-40/2001: 3-5.

Latzitis, Ninon; Sundmacher, Leonie; Busse, Reinhard (2011): Regionale Unterschiede der Lebenserwartung in Deutschland auf Ebene der Kreise und kreisfreien Städte und deren mögliche Determinanten. In: Gesundheitswesen 73,4: 217-228.

Lee, Seungil; Cho, Y.; Kim, J.; Shin, S. (2012): A Projection of Migration Flows after South-North Korea Integration and Policy Measures. Korea Institute for Health and Social Affairs (Research Report 2012-47-13). Seoul: Korea Institute for Health and Social Affairs.

Lee, Seungil; Park, S.; Nam, K.; Lee, G. (2014): A Study on Urban Development Models and Implementation Strategies for Selective North Korean Cities. Korea Research Institute for Human Settlements. Anyang: Korea Research Institute for Human Settlements.

Lee, Y.; Seo, M.; Kim, S. Suvarna; Park, Y. (2011): A Study on Infant and Child care in North Korea for the Reunification of Korea. Korea Institute of Child Care and Education. Seoul: Korea Institute of Child Care and Education.

Lehmann, Robert; Ragnitz, Joachim; May, Michaela (2010): Bilanz – 20 Jahre Deutsche Einheit. Texte zur Sozialen Marktwirtschaft 4. Berlin.

Lesthaeghe, Ron (1995): The Second Demographic Transition in Western Countries: An Interpretation. In: Mason, K. O.; Jensen, A.–M. (Eds.): Gender and Family Change in Industrialized Countries. Oxford: Clarendon Press: 17–62.

Lesthaeghe, Ron; Moors, G. (2000): Recent Trends in Fertility and Household Formation in the Industrialized World. In: Review of Population and Social Policy 9: 121–70.

Lewis, Jane (2009): Work–Family Balance, Gender and Policy. Cheltenham: Edward Elgar.

Ludwig, Udo; Stäglin, Reiner; Stahmer, Carsten (1996): Verflechtungsanalysen für die Volkswirtschaft der DDR am Vorabend der deutschen Vereinigung. (=Beiträge zur Strukturforschung, 163). Berlin.

Lück, Detlev (2015): Vaterleitbilder: Ernährer und Erzieher? In: Schneider, Norbert F.; Diabaté, Sabine; Ruckdeschel, Kerstin (Eds.): Familienleitbilder in Deutschland. Kulturelle Vorstellungen zu Partnerschaft, Elternschaft und Familienleben. Beiträge zur Bevölkerungswissenschaft 48: 227-45, Opladen: Barbara Budrich.

Lück, Detlev; Gründler, Sabine; Naderi, Robert; Dorbritz, Jürgen; Schiefer, Katrin; Ruckdeschel, Kerstin; Hiebl, Johannes; Wolfert, Sabine; Stadler, Manuela; Pupeter, Monika. (2013): Familienleitbilder 2012. Methodenbericht zur Studie. BiB Daten– und Methodenberichte 2/2013. Wiesbaden: BiB.

Luy, Marc (2004): Mortality differences between Western and Eastern Germany before and after reunification: A macro and micro level analysis of developments and responsible factors. In: Genus 60,3-4: 99-141.

Luy, Marc; Caselli, Graziella (2007): The impact of a migration-caused selection effect on regional mortality differences in Italy and Germany. In: Genus 63,1-2: 33-64.

Mai, Ralf (2004): Regionale Sterblichkeitsunterschiede in Ostdeutschland. Struktur, Entwicklung und die Ost-West-Lücke seit der Wiedervereinigung. In: Scholz, Rembrandt D.; Flöthmann, E.-Jürgen (Eds.): Lebenserwartung und Mortalität. Materialien zur Bevölkerungswissenschaft 111. Wiesbaden: Bundesinstitut für Bevölkerungsforschung: 51-68.

Martens, Bernd (2010): Zug nach Westen – Anhaltende Abwanderung: 1–7. In: Lange Wege der deutschen Einheit. bpb – Bundeszentrale für politische Bildung (Ed.): Bonn. https://www.bpb.de/geschichte/deutsche-einheit/lange-wege-der-deutschen-einheit/47253/zug-nach-westen?p=all

Mayer, Boris; Trommsdorff, Gisela (2010): Adolescents' Value of Children and Their Intentions to Have Children: A Cross–Cultural and Multilevel Analysis. In: Journal of Cross–Cultural Psychology 41,5–6: 671–89.

McCelvey, Priscilla (2016): Barriers to Integration for Refugees in South Korea. http://www.humanrightskorea.org/2016/barriers-integration-refugees-south-korea/ (last accessed 15.09.2017).

McFalls, Laurence (1995): Communism's Collapse, Democracy's Demise: The Cultural Context and Consequences of the East Germans' Revolution. New York: NYU Press et Basingstoke: Macmillan: 285 p.

Meulemann, Heiner (2002): Werte und Wertwandel im vereinten Deutschland. In: Aus Politik und Zeitgeschichte, B 37-38: 13-22.

Miller, Amanda; Sassler, Sharon (2010): Stability and Change in the Division of Labor Among Cohabiting Couples. In: Sociological Forum 25,4: 677–702.

Mons, Ute (2011): Tabakattributable Mortalität in Deutschland und in den deutschen Bundesländern. Berechnungen mit Daten des Mikrozensus und der Todesursachenstatistik. In: Gesundheitswesen 73,4: 238-246.

Mühlberg, Dietrich (2002): Schwierigkeiten kultureller Assimilation. Freuden und Mühen der Ostdeutschen beim Eingewöhnen in neue Standards des Alltagslebens. In: Aus Politik und Zeitgeschichte, B 17: 3-12.

Mühlichen, Michael (2015): Entwicklung regionaler Mortalitätsunterschiede im deutschen Ostseeraum seit der Wiedervereinigung. BiB Working Paper 5: Wiesbaden.

Myrskylä, Mikko; Scholz, Rembrandt (2013): Reversing East-West mortality difference among German women, and the role of smoking. In: International Journal of Epidemiology 42,2: 549-558.

Nauck, Bernhard (2005): Changing Value of Children: An Action Theory of Fertility Behavior and Intergenerational Relationships in Cross–Cultural Comparison. In: Friedlmeier, Wolfgang; Chakkarath, Pradeep; Schwarz, Beate (Eds.): Culture and Human Development. The Importance of Cross–Cultural Research to the Social Sciences. Hove / New York: Psychology Press: 183–202.

Nauck, Bernhard; Klaus, Daniela (2007): The Varying Value of Children: Empirical Results from Eleven Societies in Asia, Africa and Europe. In: Current Sociology 55,4: 487–503.

Nauck, Bernhard; Schneider, Norbert F.; Tölke, Angelika (Eds.) (1995): Familie und Lebensverlauf im gesellschaftlichen Umbruch. Der Mensch als soziales und personales Wesen. 12: Stuttgart: Enke.

Nolte, Ellen; Scholz, Rembrandt D.; Shkolnikov, Vladmir; McKee, Martin (2002): The contribution of medical care to changing life expectancy in Germany and Poland. In: Social Science and Medicine 55,11: 1907-1921.

Park, Chai Bin; Cho, Nam-Hoon (1995): "Consequences of Son Preference in a Low-Fertility Society: Imbalance of the Sex Ratio at Birth in Korea". In: Population and Demographic Review 21(1): 59-84.

Peukert, Christian; Smolny, Werner (2011): Interregional Migration in Germany: Characteristics and Effects for Regions and Migrants. Discussion Paper.

Pfau-Effinger, B. (2004): Socio–historical paths of the male breadwinner model – an explanation of cross–national differences. In: The British Journal of Sociology 55(3): 377–99.

Reher, David S. (2004): Family Ties in Western Europe: Persistent Contrasts. In: Gianpiero, Dalla Zuanna; Micheli, Giuseppe A. (Eds.): Strong Family and Low Fertility: A Paradox? New Perspectives in Interpreting Contemporary Family and Reproductive Behaviour. Dordrecht. Kluwer Academic Publishers: 45–76.

Reher, David. S. (1998): Family Ties in Western Europe: Persistent Contrasts. Population and development review: 203–34.

Robert-Koch-Institut (Ed.) (2011): Daten und Fakten. Ergebnisse der Studie "Gesundheit in Deutschland aktuell 2009". Beiträge zur Gesundheitsberichterstattung des Bundes. Berlin: Robert-Koch-Institut.

Robertson, Roland (1998): Glokalisierung, Homogenität und Heterogenität in Raum und Zeit. In: Ulrich Beck (Ed.): Perspektiven der Weltgesellschaft. Frankfurt a. M.: Suhrkamp: ISBN 978-3518409169: 196-220.

Ruckdeschel, Kerstin (2009): Rabenmutter contra Mère Poule: Kinderwunsch und Mutterbild im deutsch-französischen Vergleich. In: Zeitschrift für Bevölkerungswissenschaft 34,1-2: 105-134.

Sander, Nikola (2014): Internal Migration in Germany, 1995-2010: New Insights into East-West Migration and Re-urbanisation. In: Comparative Population Studies 39,2: 217-246.

Schlömer, Claus (2009): Binnenwanderungen in Deutschland zwischen Konsolidierung und neuen Paradigmen. Makroanalytische Untersuchungen zur Systematik von Wanderungsverflechtungen. Bundesinstitut für Bau-, Stadt- und Raumforschung im Bundesamt für Bauwesen und Raumordnung (Ed.). Berichte 31: Bonn.

Schlömer, Claus; Bucher, Hansjörg (2001): Arbeitslosigkeit und Binnenwanderungen: auf der Suche nach einem theoriegestützten Zusammenhang. In: Informationen zur Raumentwicklung 1: 33-47. ISSN 0303-2493.

Schneider, Norbert F. (1994): Familie und private Lebensführung in West- und Ostdeutschland. Eine vergleichende Analyse des Familienlebens 1970-1992. Soziologische Gegenwartsfragen 55: Stuttgart.

Schneider, Norbert F.; Naderi, Robert; Ruppenthal, Silvia (2012): Familie in Deutschland nach dem gesellschaftlichen Umbruch. Sind Ost-West-Differenzierungen in der Familienforschung zwanzig Jahre nach der Wiedervereinigung noch sinnvoll? In: Huinink, Johannes; Kreyenfeld, Michaela; Trappe, Heike (Eds.): Familie und Partnerschaft in Ost- und Westdeutschland. Ähnlich und doch immer noch anders. In: Zeitschrift für Familienforschung, Sonderheft 9: 29-53.

Spoorenberg, Thomas; Schwekendiek, Daniel (2012): "Demographic Changes in North Korea 1993-2008". In: Population and Development Review 38(1): 133-158.

Statistische Ämter des Bundes und der Länder (2015): 25 Jahre Deutsche Einheit. Wiesbaden

Statistisches Bundesamt (Ed.) (1990): DDR 1990 – Zahlen und Fakten: Stuttgart.

Statistisches Bundesamt (Ed.) (2000): Sonderreihe mit Beiträgen für das Gebiet der ehemaligen DDR, Heft 33: Entstehung und Verwendung des Bruttoinlandsprodukts 1970 bis 1989. Ergebnis eines von der Deutschen Forschungsgemeinschaft (DFG) geförderten Forschungsvorhabens. Wiesbaden.

Statistisches Bundesamt (2012): Periodensterbetafeln für Deutschland. Allgemeine Sterbetafeln, abgekürzte Sterbetafeln und Sterbetafeln 1871/1881 bis 2008/2010. Wiesbaden.

Statistisches Bundesamt (2016): Sterbetafeln. Ergebnisse aus der laufenden Berechnung von Periodensterbetafeln für Deutschland und die Bundesländer 2013/2015. Wiesbaden.

Statistisches Bundesamt (2017): GENESIS Pro database. Wiesbaden.

Stephen, Elizabeth Hervey (2016): "Korean Unification: a solution to the challenges of an increasingly elderly population?". In: Asian Population Studies 12(1): 50-67.

Stöbel-Richter; Yve (2010): Fertilität und Partnerschaft. Eine Längsschnittstudie zu Familien-bildungsprozessen über 20 Jahre. Gießen: Psychosozial-Verlag.

Surkyn Johan; Lesthaeghe, Ron (2004): Value Orientations and the Second Demographic Transition (SDT) in Northern, Western and Southern Europe: An Update. Demographic Research 3,3: 45–86.

United Nations (2015): DPR Korea 2015: Needs and Priorities Democratic People's Republic of Korea. United Nations Population Division. http://reliefweb.int/sites/reliefweb.int/files/resources/20150401%20DPR_Korea_NP_FINAL.pdf

United Nations (2017): World Population Prospects: The 2017 Revision. United Nations Population Division.

Van de Kaa, Dirk J. (1987): Europe's Second Demographic Transition. Population Bulletin 42,1: 3–55.

Van de Kaa, Dirk J. (1997): Opinions and Sequences: Europe's Demographic Patterns. In: Journal of Australian Population Association 14,1: 1–29.

Vaupel, James W.; Carey, James R.; Christensen, Kaare (2003): It's Never Too Late. In: Science 301: 1679-1681.

Virtala, Aira; Vilska, Sirpa; Huttunen, Teppo; Kunttu, Kristina (2011): Childbearing, the Desire to Have Children, and Awareness about the Impact of Age On Female Fertility Among Finnish University Students. In: The European Journal of Contraception and Reproductive Health Care 16,2: 108–15.

Vogt, Tobias C. (2013): How Many Years of Life Did the Fall of the Berlin Wall Add? A Projection of East German Life Expectancy. In: Gerontology 59,3: 276-282.

Vogt, Tobias C.; van Raalte, Alyson; Grigoriev, Pavel; Myrskylä, Mikko (2017): The German East-West Mortality Difference: Two Crossovers Driven by Smoking. In: Demography 54,3: 1051-1071.

Vogt, Tobias C.; Vaupel, James W. (2015): The importance of regional availability of health care for old age survival. Findings from German reunification. In: Population Health Metrics 13,26.

Vogt, Tobias; van Raalte, Alyson; Grigoriev, Pavel; Myrskylä, Mikko (2017): "The German East-West Mortality Difference: Two Crossovers Driven by Smoking". In: Demography 54(3): 1051-1071.

Wagner, Michael; Cifuentes, Isabel Valdés (2014): The Pluralisation of Living Arrangements – A Continuous Trend? In: Comparative Population Studies 39;1: 73–98.

Wehler, Hans-Ulrich (2008): Deutsche Gesellschaftsgeschichte. Fünfter Band. Bundesrepublik und DDR 1949-1990. München.

Welsch, Wolfgang (2000): Transkulturalität. Zwischen Globalisierung und Partikularisierung. In: Jahrbuch Deutsch als Fremdsprache 26. München: 327-351.

Widmer, Eric; Jallinoja, Riitta (Eds.) (2008): Beyond the Nuclear Family: Families in a Configurational Perspective. Bern: Peter Lang.

Wolfgang Weiß (2006): Zur Entwicklung einer Residualbevölkerung infolge lang anhaltender selektiver Abwanderung in Mecklenburg-Vorpommern – Auswirkungen der Bevölkerungsalterung unter besonderer Berücksichtigung regionaler Aspekte In: Zeitschrift für Bevölkerungswissenschaft 31,3-4: 469-506. Wiesbaden: VS Verlag für Sozialwissenschaften. ISSN: 0340-2398.

Yoo, Sam Hyun; Hayford, Sarah R.; Agadjanian, Victor (2017): "Old Habits Die Hard? Lingering Son Preference in an Era of Normalizing Sex Ratios at Birth in South Korea". In: Population Research and Policy Review 36(1): 25-54.

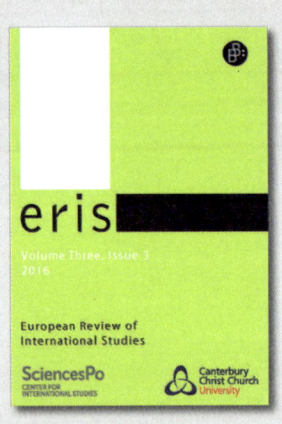

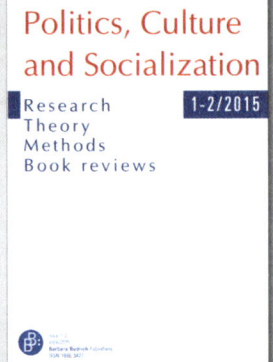